The Southwest for Free

Also by the authors:

Europe on 10 Salads a Day
Bet On It! The Ultimate Guide to Nevada

Also in this series:

Europe for Free
by Brian Butler

Hawaii for Free
by Frances Carter

London for Free
by Brian Butler

DC for Free
by Brian Butler

Paris for Free
(Or Extremely Cheap)
by Mark Beffart

THE
SOUTHWEST
FOR FREE

REVISED EDITION

Hundreds
of Free Things
to Do in the
Southwest U.S.

GREG & MARY JANE EDWARDS

Mustang Publishing
Memphis, TN

For Emily

Maps and illustrations by Claire Stamatien.

Note: Maps are not drawn to scale.

Library of Congress Cataloging-in-Publication Data
Edwards, Greg, 1940-
      The Southwest for free : hundreds of free things to do in the southwest U.S. / Greg & Mary Jane Edwards. -- Rev. ed.
      p.   cm.
      ISBN 0-914457-83-7 (alk. paper)
      1. Southwest, New--Guidebooks.   I. Edwards, Mary Jane, 1938-   .   II. Title.
F785.3.E37   1997
917.904'33--dc21   96-49223
                                                           CIP

Printed on acid-free paper.
10 9 8 7 6 5 4 3 2 1

CONTENTS

Introduction 8

ARIZONA •••11

Ajo • 13

Apache Junction • 14

Bisbee • 14

Bullhead City • 15

Camp Verde • 15

Casa Grande • 15

Chinle • 17

Douglas • 17

Flagstaff • 18

Florence • 19

Fort Huachuca • 19

Ganado • 20

Globe • 21

Jerome • 21

Kingman • 22

Lake Havasu City • 24

Navajo National
     Monument • 26

Nogales • 26

Page • 27

Parker • 28

Phoenix • 29

Prescott • 33

Quartzsite • 34

Sacaton • 35

Sedona • 35

Thatcher • 37

Tombstone • 37

Tubac • 38

Tucson • 39

Wickenburg • 46

Willcox • 47

Window Rock • 48

Yuma • 48

NEVADA •••51

Austin • 55

Beatty • 56

Boulder City • 56

Caliente • 57

Carson City • 59

Elko • 60

Ely • 62

Eureka • 64

Fallon • 64

Gabbs • 65

Genoa • 65

Goldfield • 66

Hawthorne • 66

Henderson • 67

Las Vegas • 68

Laughlin • 72

Lovelock • 73

Overton • 73

Pioche • 74

Rachel • 75

Reno • 75

Sparks • 77

Tahoe • 77

Tonopah • 78

Virginia City • 79

Wells • 80

Winnemucca • 81

NEW MEXICO ••• 83

Abiquiu • 88

Acoma • 88

Alamogordo • 89

Albuquerque • 90

Angel Fire • 96

Artesia • 97

Carlsbad • 97

Chimayo • 98

Cimarron • 99

Cloudcroft • 99

Cochiti • 100

Deming • 101

Dulce • 102

Española • 102

Gallup • 103

Grants • 103

Hobbs • 104

Las Cruces • 104

Las Vegas • 105

Los Alamos • 106

Raton • 107

Roswell • 108

Santa Fe • 108

Silver City • 112

Socorro • 115

Taos • 117

Brigham City • 125

Castle Dale • 125

Cedar City • 126

Delta • 128

Gouldings • 128

Green River • 128

Helper • 129

Hovenweep National
   Monument • 129

Kanab • 130

Logan • 130

Moab • 131

Ogden • 132

Park City • 133

Price • 134

Provo • 135

Richfield • 137

Roosevelt • 138

Salt Lake City • 138

Springville • 146

St. George • 147

Vernal • 149

INTRODUCTION

The Southwest United States is renowned for its history, scenery, and American Indian culture, but few of its millions of visitors know there are hundreds of things to see and do that are absolutely **free**.

The Southwest for Free will help visitors and residents discover state parks, art galleries, fiestas, historic homes, battlefields, gardens, churches, and much more. And every place listed is free at least one day a week.

The book is organized alphabetically by state and then by city. If a place is too tiny to be called a town, we've included it in the section under the nearest city or village. The entries give background information on the town, admission days and hours, addresses and phone numbers, and the address and phone number of the local Chamber of Commerce, should you want to make advance travel plans.

At press time, all the information in this guide was correct. However, remember that things change, and you should verify hours and admission policies before you arrive.

We welcome your comments and suggestions for future editions of *The Southwest for Free*. Please write to us in care of Mustang Publishing, Box 3004, Memphis, TN 38173 USA.

Greg & Mary Jane Edwards

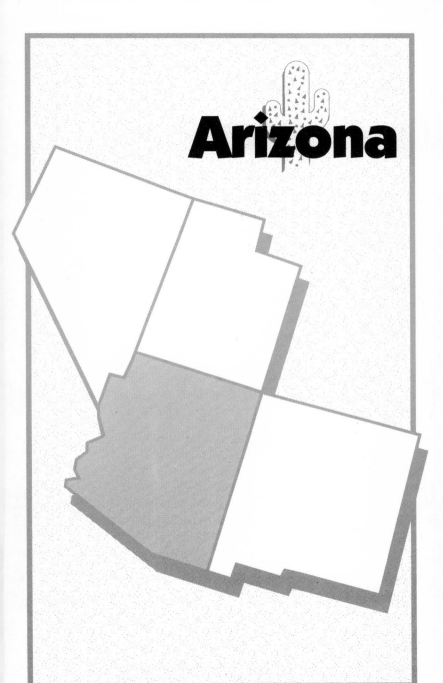

Arizona

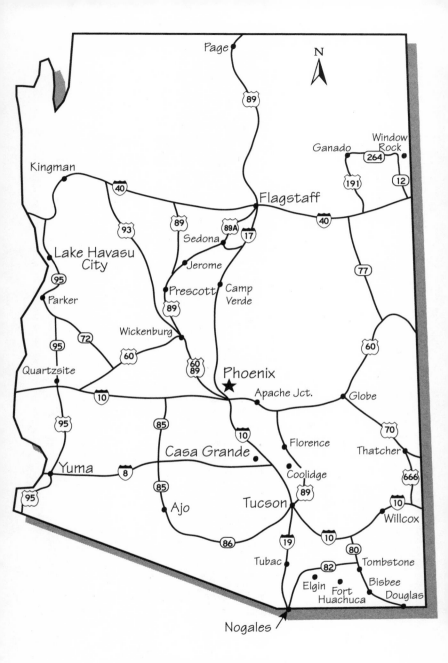

ARIZONA

Arizona

It's easy to get the wrong idea about Arizona: that it's just a sleepy, sun-baked desert state with a *siesta* mentality. After all, it borders Mexico, and it's full of sand and cactus.

But look around Arizona and you'll find a land of contrasts. Few states have such spectacular terrain. From the depths of the Grand Canyon in the north to the heights of Mt. Lemmon in the south, the diversity is dramatic. The mountains are lush and backed by high, forbidding cliffs. Rugged, snow-capped peaks and steep gorges with rushing waterfalls loom above the most enchanting desert on earth. The Colorado River zigzags through deep ravines into the Grand Canyon, flows west into Lake Mead (the largest manmade body of water in the U.S.), and turns south to mark the boundary with California. The Sonora desert region is ridged by heavily forested mountains, where the palo verde gives way to the pine. East of the wild beauty of the Grand Canyon lies the shining kaleidoscope of the Painted Desert.

Arizona offers an endless medley to its travelers, a place bursting with sunsets and saguaro, where cowboys still ride the plains and travelers find prehistoric Indian dwellings and centuries-old civilizations nestled close to modern art museums and shopping malls.

Historians say humans first settled in Arizona over 12,000 years ago. Ruins speak of the Anasazi and Hohokam tribes, as well as the early Navajos and Apaches. The reservations still echo the rhythms of dances unchanged for generations. Spanish explorers came from Mexico in the early 1500's, followed by Jesuit priests, who established missions throughout the Southwest.

Arizona was the only territory west of Texas to join the Confederacy during the Civil War. The capital changed locations several times, from Prescott to Tucson and finally to Phoenix. In 1912, Arizona became the 48th state.

Prospectors and their burros made mining the chief source of Arizona's income decades ago, but that's been surpassed by tourism and manufacturing. However, miners' ghost towns still live, as nostalgia for frontier history and a laissez-faire lifestyle keep the Old West alive in places like Douglas and Bisbee. You can see a reenactment of the shootout at the O.K. Corral in Tombstone and wild donkeys roaming the town of Oatman. The first European settlement in what is now Arizona is at Tubac, an art colony just outside Tucson. The state prides itself on its Western and Indian art, displayed in first-class galleries.

The dry, sunny climate and the abundance of scenery contribute to the state's reputation as an ideal place to visit, and many visitors return to live, especially for retirement. Tourists arrive in all seasons, spending as much time outdoors as possible. There's always great weather somewhere for bicycling, fishing, camping, golf, tennis, rockhounding, or stargazing.

For rock hounds, Arizona is a dream come true; you can spend a few days or the rest of your life searching for petrified wood, quartz, amethyst, opals, and turquoise. In February, Quartzsite hosts a huge rock and mineral show—and the town's population grows from 2,000 to a million people. In Apache Junction, the legend of the Lost Dutchman Mine lives on, celebrated by those who still hope to find the fortune said to be hidden in the nearby Superstition Mountains.

Arizona's museums reflect its diversity, too. Tour the nation's oldest surviving cavalry post at Fort Huachuca, or visit the Kitt Peak Observatory, site of the world's largest solar telescope. The Navajo and Hopi nations welcome visitors to some ceremonies and encourage sightseeing. Window Rock, the head-quarters of the Navajo nation, celebrates its heritage each September with a powwow and performances of traditional dances and songs. Yuma, on the Colorado River, is the gateway to California and the 26,000-acre Imperial Wildlife refuge. There are challenging, high-altitude trails for hikers near Flagstaff, and just south of Sedona is red rock country, a glowing fantasy land of rocky crags, spires, and arches.

Sometime in spring — just when depends on the winter rains — the desert explodes into bloom, splashing the landscape with a stunning display of purple, pink, red, yellow, and white. But heed a few cautions if you venture out to look at the cactus flowers. First, dress wisely with leather (not cloth) shoes and long pants that cover the ankles. Don't touch cactus; cholla breaks off easily and pieces on the ground can latch onto unprotected ankles. Be careful not to trample tiny desert plants or shallow cactus roots. Wear sun block and sunglasses. Finally, don't wander far from your car, and *always* carry water with you, at least a gallon per person.

Sun-baked deserts and snowy mountain peaks, forests in a thousand shades of green and high grassy plains, painted canyons and rushing rivers, prehistoric ruins and modern cities, sports and art, cowboys and Indians — Arizona offers an unmatched diversity.

AJO

A desert community 43 miles north of the Mexican border, Ajo is known for having the best climate in the country. It's designed in the Spanish tradition, with a center courtyard adorned with palms and tiled benches for relaxing.

A nearby **open-pit mine** extends over a mile in diameter; you can observe it from a lookout point on SR 85. The **Cabeza Prieta Wildlife Refuge** is just outside Ajo. The 860,000-acre refuge protects desert wildlife like lizards and kangaroo rats, as well as endangered species like the Sonoran antelope. Headquarters is at 1611 N. Second Ave., and you must have an entry permit issued at the visitors center. Open Mon-Fri 7:30am-4:30pm (phone 520-387-6483).

APACHE JUNCTION

East of Apache Junction lie the **Superstition Mountains**, named for the legends told about them and the Lost Dutchman Gold Mine, which remains hidden among the peaks and valleys. The mine was named after Jacob Waltz, a shadowy character who claimed to have discovered it around 1868. He periodically produced bags of gold nuggets, which he spent in the local saloons. Though many different tales exist about the mine, one thing is certain: if there was ever any gold, it's still there, and at least eight men have lost their lives searching for it. Each February, the town celebrates with **Lost Dutchman Days**, a festival with concerts, a parade, and a carnival. The Chamber of Commerce can be reached at Box 1747, Apache Junction, AZ 85217 (phone 520-982-3141).

Outside of town, **Fish Creek Canyon** is worth seeing for its brilliantly colored walls rising 2,000 feet above the highway.

BISBEE

To stop in Bisbee is to stop in time. The quaint little mining town lies in the Mule Mountains, 100 miles southeast of Tucson, and has retained its charm. Its well-preserved, turn-of-the-century structures are full of Old West history and mining lore. In 1892, Phelps Dodge began mining there, and Bisbee became the biggest city in Arizona for a time. Eventually the copper ran out, and many of the people left, only to be replaced by artists who came to restore and preserve the town.

Bisbee is built into the sides of the mountains, with many small houses hanging precariously over the ravines. The town is filled with artsy shops, restaurants, and galleries. The **Bisbee Historical Society Museum** at 37 Main St. maintains Bisbee's past with memorabilia, old clothing, and period furnishings.

The cactus story is one of the most amazing of natural history, and the **Arizona Cactus and Succulent Research Center** at 8 Cactus Lane maintains an extensive library of information, books, reports, and photos about these desert plants. Samples of over 750 varieties of high desert plant life are grown, and guided tours of the garden are available at all times. Open sunrise to sunset daily (phone 520-432-7040).

While Bisbee hosts many events through the year, the most famous is the **Vuelta de Bisbee**, a U.S. Cycling Federation race in the last weekend in April. The grueling, four-day competition fills the town to capacity with spectators, who enjoy the race and many other events. Bisbee also supports a lively cultural scene with concerts, art exhibitions, and theater.

The Chamber of Commerce can be reached at Box BA, Bisbee, AZ 85603 (phone 520-432-5421). The Chamber has two tour maps: an art and antiques walk and a self-guided walking tour of the historic commercial district. Just strolling the old streets of Bisbee is an adventure in itself.

BULLHEAD CITY

Each April in Riverview Park, Bullhead City hosts the Arizona State Championship Chili Cook-Off, featuring cooks from all over the country. Music, a costume contest, arts and crafts booths, and, of course, free samples, add to the fun. For more information, call 520-763-5885.

Rockhounds will love the Silvery Colorado River Rock Gemboree held each April at the Junior High School, 1062 Hancock Rd. The fair features over 50 displays, plus silversmithing and faceting demonstrations.

CAMP VERDE

Founded in 1866 to defend settlers from Apache Indian raids, Camp Verde is today the site of the **Yavapai-Apache Center**, which offers a slide presentation on the area's prehistoric residents and exhibits on the ancient and contemporary lifestyles of area Indians. Allow at least two hours to see everything. Open daily Memorial Day-Oct. 31 from 8am-6pm; from 8am-5pm the remainder of the year (phone 520-567-5276).

CASA GRANDE

An hour north of Tucson, Casa Grande is named for the **Hohokam Indian Ruins** 20 miles northeast of town. The ruins were built over 650 years ago of caliche mud, and you can

The ruins of the main building at Casa Grande.
(Photo: Richard Frear)

tour remains of prehistoric villages found around the four-story main building. The visitors center offers interpretive exhibits. Open daily 7am-6pm throughout the year, including holidays (1100 Ruins Dr., Coolidge, AZ 85228; phone 520-723-3172).

Near Casa Grande just off Hwy. 10, **Picacho Peak State Park** was the site of the only Civil War battle fought in the Arizona Territory. Each year in March, members of the Arizona Civil War Council and the 7th Confederate Cavalry stage a reenactment. In the spring, the park, covered with wildflowers, becomes a photographer's paradise. For details, call the Park at 520-466-3183.

Nearly 7,000 feet above sea level, **Kitt Peak National Observatory** off Hwy. 86 is home to the Robert R. McMath Solar

Telescope, the world's largest, and a 158-inch stellar telescope used to monitor the sun by day and the stars by night. There's a picnic area but no food facilities. Films run daily at 10:30am and 1:30pm, and guided tours are available in the afternoons. Open daily 10am-4pm (phone 520-327-5511).

O'Odham Tash, which means "gathering of the people," is a four-day festival each February in Casa Grande. Though only Indians may compete in the events, everyone can find something to see and do—traditional ceremonial dances, pow-wows, arts and crafts exhibits, parades of Indian marching bands, and the Queen's Pageant.

The Casa Grande Chamber of Commerce is at 575 N. Marshall, Casa Grande, AZ 85222 (phone 520-836-2125).

CHINLE

One of the largest archaeological monuments in the U.S., the **Canyon de Chelly National Monument** displays an amazing collection of red rock cliffs, sandstone spires, prehistoric pictographs, and cliff dwellings dating from A.D. 900. You'll also find many hiking trails and two scenic drives. For more information, contact the National Monument at P.O. Box 588, Chinle, AZ 86503 (phone 520-674-5500).

DOUGLAS

Douglas, a little town known as the "Gateway to Mexico," was built mostly in the early 1900's. Be sure to see the **Gadsden Hotel** at 1046 G Ave., built in 1906, with a lobby featuring a leaded stained glass mural 42 feet long, an Italian white marble staircase, and Tiffany vaulted skylights.

Church Square is the only block in the world where a church rests on each of the four corners. Four denominations are represented—Methodist, Episcopalian, Baptist, and Presbyterian—and each church was built before 1908.

The Douglas **Fiesta Patrias Celebration** honors its Mexican neighbor each Sept. 16, Mexico's Independence Day, and the **Two Flags Festival of the Arts** runs every October. Each has art exhibits, parades, a chili cook-off, and ethnic food. A grand ball highlights the Two Flags Festival, with a queen and princess chosen each year to wear the traditional costumes.

In February at the annual **gun show**, you can "buy, sell, swap, or just look at" rare old guns, knives, and western memorabilia. It's held at the Cochise County fairgrounds on Leslie Canyon Rd.

The address for the Douglas Chamber of Commerce is 1125 Pan American, Douglas, AZ 85607 (phone 520-364-2477).

FLAGSTAFF

The Anasazi ("ancient ones") settled the Flagstaff area long before Coronado came seeking the legendary Seven Cities of Gold. Surrounded by the largest Ponderosa forest in the nation, Flagstaff derived its name from a single pine stripped of its branches and raised on Independence Day in 1876 to serve as a trail marker for the wagon trains headed for California. A pamphlet describing a **self-guided driving tour** past the many scenic attractions near Flagstaff is available at the Chamber of Commerce, 1 E. SR66, Flagstaff, AZ 86001 (phone 520-774-4505 or 800-842-7293).

Northern Arizona University offers **observatory tours** from 7:30pm-10pm on Thursdays. The observatory is north of the Skydome (phone 520-523-7170). The University also offers art exhibitions at the **Old Main Art Museum and Gallery** (phone 520-523-3471).

The Arboretum, the highest botanical garden in the United States, lies in a beautiful wooded area on Woody Mountain Rd. off Hwy. 66, southwest of Flagstaff. Native Arizona plants and flowers are displayed alongside rare species. Open 10am-3pm Mon-Fri (phone 520-774-1441).

In February, the annual **Flagstaff Winter Festival** features a range of events — sled dog races, cross-country skiing, a barn dance, a story fest, live music, a winter stargaze, wine-tasting, and snow games. There's even an event called Frozen Buns Fun Run! Call toll free 800-842-7293 for information. May brings a **folk arts program**, "Trappings of the American West," which celebrates the lifestyle of the cowboys. In June, the annual **Festival of Native American Artists** offers films, an outdoor Indian market, Native American dances, a guided nature walk, and a food demonstration. Both celebrations are held at the Coconino Center for the Arts on North Fort Valley Rd. (which is Fort Valley Rd. in town but becomes Hwy. 180 outside of town and leads to the Grand Canyon). Phone 520-779-6921 for details.

FLORENCE

Florence is one of Arizona's oldest towns, founded in 1866, and many of its old buildings have a frontier flavor. The **Pinal County Historical Museum** at 715 S. Main St. (phone 520-868-4382) has Indian artifacts from the Southwest and Mexico, antiques, blacksmith tools, a barbed wire display, and letters and photos depicting the county's history. There's even a restored homesteader's shack on display. Open Wed-Sun 11am-4pm from July 16-Aug 31 and Dec 1-April 6. The rest of the year, the hours are noon-4pm.

On the first Saturday after Thanksgiving, Florence holds the **Florence Junior Parade**, one of the oldest junior rodeos and parades in the nation. Information on the rodeo and other local points of interest is available at the Pinal County Visitor Center, located in a territorial home at 912 Pinal St., Florence, AZ 85232 (phone 520-868-4331). Open daily 10am-2pm.

FORT HUACHUCA

Eighty years before the Pilgrims came to Plymouth Rock, Coronado of Spain marched through what is now Cochise County, looking for the fabled "Seven Cities of Cíbola," each supposedly built of gold. His search paved the way for other explorers, and the many Indian tribes in the area were forced to band together against the foreigners. The area's Apaches held off the Spaniards and then the Mexicans for over 300 years.

Fort Huachuca is the only post surviving of the 50 established to provide protection for the settlers. After the Apaches were quelled, miners discovered gold, silver, and copper near-by, and towns sprang up nearly overnight.

The fort, now headquarters of the U.S. Army Information Systems Command and the U.S. Army Intelligence Center, is the oldest active surviving cavalry post. Built in 1877, it covers over 73,000 acres. The **Fort Huachuca Museum**, three miles northwest of the main gate at Boyd and Grierson Avenues, traces the history of the Southwest and the army's relation to it. You must get a visitor's pass at the main gate; show your driver's license and proof of auto registration. Open Mon-Fri 9am-4pm and Sat & Sun 1pm-4pm. Closed on federal holidays. Phone 520-533-5736.

Sierra Vista hosts an annual **Winter Arts Festival** in late January at the Yrun Community Center, 3020 E. Tacoma Ave. Well-known artists and local talent are part of the program, which attracts hundreds of participants. Call 520-458-7922 for more information on dates and times.

GANADO

Considered sovereign nations, Indian reservations make and enforce their own laws. Before you visit Ganado or any reservation, know the following rules: alcoholic beverages are not permitted; leaving the road and hiking across the country is prohibited; drivers and passengers must wear seat belts, and cyclists must wear helmets; and the Navajo Reservation is the only place in the state that observes daylight saving time.

Just west of Ganado is the oldest continually operating **trading post** on the Navajo reservation. John Hubbell, one of the leading traders of the era, established it in 1878, and its business today is conducted in much the same way. Rangers offer guided tours of the trading post and the Hubbell family home, and members of the Navajo, Hopi, and Zuni tribes sell and trade rugs, baskets, jewelry, and pottery.

The visitors center has a brochure depicting a self-guided tour, plus daily demonstrations of weaving and silversmithing. Allow at least two hours to see everything. Open daily 8am-6pm June-Sept; 8am-5pm the rest of the year. For details, contact Hubbell Trading Post National Historic Site, Box 150, Ganado, AZ 86505 (phone 520-755-3475).

GLOBE

Globe is the eastern end of the scenic highway called the **Apache Trail**, home to gunfighters, Apaches, and silver. The area was a favorite stop for the likes of Bat Masterson, Wyatt Earp, and Doc Holliday, and it has been home to the Apaches for hundreds of years. Silver brought the desperados, but copper is the real treasure, still being mined today. Nearby, **Devil's Canyon**, west on Hwy. 60, is known for its cathedral-like towers of stone. The Queen Creek gorge, bridge, and tunnel are all on the drive through the canyon.

The rip-roaring mining days of Globe are brought to life in the **Gila County Historical Museum**, which also displays artifacts from the Besh-ba-Gowah ruins that were inhabited from 1225-1400 by the Salado Indians. The museum, next to the Chamber of Commerce on Hwy. 60, is open Mon-Fri 10am-4pm (phone 520-425-7385).

At the **Cobre Valley Center for the Arts** (open Mon-Sat 9am-5pm and Sun 1pm-5pm), you'll see a wide variety of arts and crafts produced by local artists in many different media. Volunteers from the center are restoring many of Globe's elegant old buildings. Phone 520-425-0884.

The Chamber of Commerce has a brochure about a driving tour of the old copper mines. There's also a walking tour of the historic buildings in downtown Globe.

In April, Globe celebrates its heritage with **Copper Dust Stampede Days**, a celebration that includes a parade, dancing, and a barbecue. **Apache Day** is held each October with Native American food, arts, and clothing.

The Globe Chamber of Commerce is at 1360 Broad St., Globe, AZ 85502 (phone 520-425-4495).

JEROME

Though tiny, Jerome is a real town, not a ghost town, full of history and mining tales. Plan to spend an entire day to walk around, the best way to see it. The mines closed in 1955, but new people moved in, and today the village is a thriving artists' community. Jerome clings to the side of a mountain, a mile into the sky. The **Mine Museum** on Main Street has mine artifacts from Jerome's past. It's open daily from 9am-4:30pm (closed Christmas, New Year's, and Thanksgiving).

In February there's a **chili cook-off**, in June an **Astronomy Festival**, and in July a **Kid's Art Cardboard Parade**. And for two weeks around Christmas, the town becomes a fairyland of lights. In Clarkdale, on the road to Jerome, the **Arizona Botanical Gardens** offers the desert in bloom all year. On Hwy. 89A, the gardens are open daily 9am-6pm (phone 520-634-2166).

Jerome is tiny, and so is its Chamber of Commerce, but if you have questions, a friendly someone will answer if you write to the Jerome Chamber of Commerce, P.O. Drawer K, Jerome, AZ 86331 (phone 520-634-5716).

KINGMAN

The main stop on the longest surviving stretch of historic Highway 66, Kingman is surrounded by ghost towns evoking an image of gunslingers, saloons, and ladies of the evening. Kingman was settled by Edward Beale, who surveyed a wagon route to California. (He's best remembered, however, for using camels in the survey parties.) In 1890, the railroad was completed to Kingman; the line later became the Atchison, Topeka, and the Santa Fe. Today in **Locomotive Park**, you'll find a miniature outdoor transportation museum complete with a colorful caboose and the last steam engine to run through Kingman.

The **Bonelli House** on 5th and Spring Streets, a "mansion from the past," is maintained by the city of Kingman. It is characteristic of the territorial architecture popular in Arizona in the late 1800's. Some of the furnishings are the original possessions of the Bonelli family, and the home is on the National Register of Historic Places. Open Thur-Mon from 1pm-5pm; closed major holidays.

The best way to experience Kingman's history is with a self-guided tour detailed in a brochure naming 24 historic spots.

Get it at the Chamber of Commerce, 333 W. Andy Devine Rd., Kingman, AZ 86402 (phone 520-753-6106).

Andy Devine, a cowboy actor, was a native of Kingman, and the city celebrates **Andy Devine Days** each year in September with a parade, cook-out, and rodeo. For more Devine lore, the **Hotel Beale**, once owned by the Devine family, is open to the public and displays memorabilia honoring the actor and his family. Movie buffs will also want to visit the Beale to see where Clark Gable and Carole Lombard honeymooned after being married in Kingman.

Two nearby "living" ghost towns draw thousands of visitors each year. **Oatman**, a short but winding 26 miles southeast on historic Hwy. 66, is set in the stunning Black Mountains in the middle of craggy rock pinnacles. The road is itself an adventure, running through narrow passes and steep cliffs and then spiraling toward the floor of the Mojave Desert. As picturesque as a Wild West movie set, Oatman's **Main Street** is lined with authentic dusty wooden buildings, board sidewalks, remnants of mining shafts, and saloons. Wild burros, descendants of the donkeys that belonged to the miners who built Oatman in 1906, roam the streets as if they owned the town. When the mines closed, the burros were left behind and soon adapted to the area, learning to live on the handouts from travelers passing through on Route 66.

Among the tourists were many Hollywood celebrities, who stayed at the **Oatman Hotel**, now on the National Register and open 8am-10pm daily. On Labor Day weekend, Oatman stages **Gold Camp Days**, with parades, a haystack scramble for the kids, hat and beard contests, an international "burro biscuit"-throwing contest, and Wild West "shootouts."

The old silver-mining town of **Chloride** is a 20-minute drive northwest of Kingman, four miles off Hwy. 93. Some of the original buildings still stand: the old bank vault is a museum, and the Tennessee Saloon is now a general store. Each April, the town hosts **Black Powder Days**, featuring shooting competitions, music, vaudeville shows, and "gunfights" staged by the Immortal Gunfighters of Chloride. On the last Saturday in June,

Chloride holds an **Old Miners Day**, starting with a pancake breakfast, a parade at noon, and a street dance at night. A trailer park lets self-contained units park free.

The **Hualapai Indians** control a million acres along a 100-mile stretch of the south rim of the Grand Canyon. A 15-minute drive leads you to **Hualapai Mountain Park**, where you'll find huge ponderosa pine, cedar, aspen, mountain mahogany, maple, and oak. The park is called a "biological island," since it's not attached to any mountain chain. Animal life abounds; expect to see mule deer, elk, raccoon, fox, golden eagles, and a variety of hummingbirds. Six miles of undeveloped but well-maintained trail leads to the peaks and offers spectacular views of the surrounding countryside.

LAKE HAVASU CITY

Forty-five miles long, Lake Havasu is part of the Colorado River, and as such supplies water to Los Angeles and cities along the way. It also provides a stunning setting for the resort city of the same name. The town got the world's attention when Robert McCulloch, who owned much of the surrounding land, purchased the **London Bridge** and had it moved to Lake Havasu. The bridge, which once spanned the Thames River in London, was transported block by block from England and reassembled in its original form. In early October each year, residents commemorate the 1971 dedication with a week-long celebration called **London Bridge Days**. In late November, crowds gather to watch the **Havasu Classic Outboard World Championships**, an international boating event, and in December, the **Christmas Boat Parade of Lights** is held beneath the bridge.

Be sure to walk down cobblestone **Shambles Lane** under London Bridge, an authentic reproduction of the Shambles of York. Peek into the windows of the "shoppes," and visit the **London Bridge Candle Factory**, where they make candles while you watch. The aroma is heavenly.

Indian tribes make their homes on nearby reservations and proudly display their culture in annual powwows. In **Topock**

London Bridge now spans Lake Havasu.

Gorge, south of the junction of I-40 and the Colorado River, ancient storytelling lives on in petroglyphs. The Gorge is also home to the **Havasu National Wildlife Refuge**, accessible only by boat or on foot. The 46,000-acre park is home to one of America's rarest birds, the Yuma clapper rail. The refuge also shelters bighorn sheep, beaver, and migratory birds. It's open daily 8am-4pm (phone 619-326-3853).

The Lake Havasu Chamber of Commerce is at 1930 Mesquite Ave., Suite 3, Lake Havasu City, AZ 86403 (phone 520-453-3444 or 800-242-8278).

NAVAJO NATIONAL MONUMENT

In northeast Arizona, the Navajo National Monument protects some of the Southwest's largest and best-preserved Anasazi cliff dwellings. From the visitors center, a half-mile trail descends to the Betatakin Ruins overlook, where you'll see stone houses crowd a ledge beneath a high alcove. The walls of the houses are intact, as are many of the roofs. Bits of ancient pottery litter the ground, and the granaries are filled with 700-year-old corncobs.

For a fee, rangers lead tours of two dwellings from the 13th century—although the tours aren't for the faint-of-heart! One tour requires a five-mile hike with some very steep stretches; the other is a 17-mile trek on horseback with a Navajo guide.

The National Monument has campgrounds and places for picnics. Call 520-672-2366 for more information.

NOGALES

A port of entry to Mexico, Nogales is rich in Spanish and Mexican history. The **Pimeria Alta Historical Society Museum,** at 136 N. Grand Ave., has displays that tell of the history of southern Arizona and northern Mexico, from the days of the Hohokam Indians to the present. You'll see Indian artifacts and pioneer household items, along with a research library. Open Mon-Fri 9am-5pm and Sat 10am-4pm (closed on major holidays) (phone 520-287-4621).

If you'd like a taste of another culture, walk across the border into Mexico. You don't need a passport to walk over, but if you plan on driving into the country, you'll need a tourist card. In Nogales, Mexico, you'll find colorful shops selling many handicrafts, including clothing, rugs, leather goods, silver, and glassware. In early May, catch the **Cinco de Mayo Festival** commemorating Mexico's defeat of Napoleon in 1862.

Nineteen miles northeast of Nogales, Arizona, the tiny village of **Patagonia** is home to the Nature Conservancy's **Patagonia-Sonoita Creek Preserve**, one of the premier bird-watching sites in the U.S. The visitors center contains an open-air pavilion that lets you feel the wind and watch the hawks overhead while you peruse the interpretive panels. A half-mile self-guided nature trail, accessible to the disabled, is great for those who want to see some of the preserve without walking the entire 2.5-mile network of trails. Open Wed-Sun 7:30am-4pm; closed holidays (phone 520-304-2400).

Patagonia's **Santa Cruz Winery** on Hwy. 82 is the only kosher vintner in Arizona. Founded in 1992, the winery can produce 5,000 gallons a year from the grapes grown on its own terra rosa vineyards. Its wines are produced under the supervision of a rabbi from Tucson. Open for tastings Thur-Sun 11am-5pm (phone 520-394-2888).

Another area winery, **Arizona Vineyards**, features 11 varieties of filtered country wines. They produce 50,000 gallons annually and bottle four times a year. Open for tastings 10am-5pm daily. (In the European tradition, if you want to sample or buy the wine, you must tour the winery.) 1830 Patagonia Rd., phone 520-287-7972.

PAGE

John Page, the town's namesake, was instrumental in the development of the upper Colorado River. Page is a center for those who wish to take a trip into the **Glen Canyon Recreation Area** or a scenic flight over **Lake Powell**.

Page is probably best known for **Rainbow Bridge**, in the Glen Canyon Recreation Area of Utah — one of the Seven Natural Wonders of the World and one of the Navajo Nation's sacred places. It's the world's largest natural bridge, almost 300 feet high and 275 feet wide. The sandstone arch on top is immense, and with the arch below, the formation truly resembles an earthbound rainbow. You can reach the bridge after hiking 13 miles through some rugged terrain or by taking a boat and then a quarter-mile hike. (Boat tours leave regularly from Bullfrog Marina on Lake Powell, but there's a charge for the ride.)

The **Glen Canyon Recreation Area** runs along the Colorado River in southeast Utah to Grand Canyon National Park. The area contains Lake Powell, the second-largest reservoir in

North America — 200 miles long, with over 2,000 miles of shoreline. Lake Powell is ringed by hidden canyons and red cliffs, but you'll find sandy beaches as well, plus many water sports. The **Carl Hayden Visitors Center** at Glen Canyon has a self-guided tour of the dam.

The **John Wesley Powell Museum,** at Lake Powell Blvd. and North Navajo Dr., has exhibits relating to the nearby Indian culture, the geology of the Colorado, and the life of Powell, the river's first modern-day explorer and scientist. Films depicting historic figures and nearby destinations are shown upon request. Open 8am-6pm Mon-Sat (phone 520-645-9496).

PARKER

The 11-mile strip of the Colorado River between Parker Dam and the Headgate Rock forms one of the finest bodies of water for water sports in Arizona.

The **Colorado River Indian Tribes Museum** in Parker is a trading center for the nearby Indian towns. The museum, at 2nd Ave. and Mojave Rd., houses a famous basket collection and artifacts from the restoration of the ghost town of La Paz. Four tribes are represented: Mojave, Chemehuevi, Navajo, and Hopi, each with its own distinct language, culture, and tradition.

The Mojave ties to the area date to prehistoric times, and the tribe is known for its skill in beadwork. The Chemehuevi, closely related to the Paiutes of Nevada, are famous for basket weaving, the finest in the Southwest. The Hopi make beautiful pottery, jewelry, and carved *kachina* dolls. The Navajo migrated to the Southwest in the early 1500's, hunting game and gathering wild plants. The art of the Navajo is silversmithing, and they are known world-wide for their intricate rug-weaving, still practiced by the women of the reservation. The museum is open 8am-5pm Mon-Fri, closed Sat, Sun, and holidays (phone 520-669-9211, ext. 335).

The **Parker Dam and Power Plant** is 12 miles northeast of town on SR 95. The dam is the world's deepest, with 65% of its structure below the Colorado River bed. Short recorded talks, illustrated maps, and close views make the self-guided tour quite entertaining. The dam creates a reservoir—from which water can be pumped into the river and the Arizona aqueducts—that can store nearly 211 billion gallons. The power plant is open from 8am-5pm daily.

The **Balloon Fest** in March offers rides, a parade, dances, sky divers, and barbecue. The events begin at 7am.

The Parker Chamber of Commerce is at Box 627, Parker, AZ 85344 (phone 520-669-2174).

PHOENIX

Phoenix, the ninth largest city in the U.S., is the capital of Arizona. Its Southwestern architecture, Native American influences, sophisticated lifestyle, and climate ideal for outdoor activities make it a first-rate place to visit.

Phoenix features three great free museums. The **Arizona Museum**, at 1002 W. Van Buren St., depicts 2,000 years of state history, including the life of the Hohokam Indians and the English settlements prior to 1912. The museum is open 11am-4pm Wed-Sun, closed major holidays (phone 602-253-2734). The **Arizona Mining and Mineral Museum** displays industrial minerals and gems found in Arizona. Exhibits also discuss all phases of Earth science (1502 Washington St.; open Mon-Fri 8am-5pm & Sat 1pm-5pm, closed holidays; phone 602-255-3791). The **Arizona State Capital Museum,** at 1700 W. Washington St., opened in 1900 and served as the territorial capital until Arizona was admitted to the Union in 1912. The restored wings contain political memorabilia and changing exhibits on state history. Guided tours are given Mon-Fri at 10am and 2pm. The legislative galleries adjoin the capital and are open Mon-Fri 8am-5pm (phone 602-542-4675).

Encanto Park, at North 15th Ave. and W. Encanto Blvd., features a lagoon and islands serving as a waterfowl refuge. Nature trails abound, and there are tennis, basketball, and volleyball courts. Open daily from sunrise to 12:30am.

Heritage Square at 6th and Monroe Streets has Victorian architecture representative of the original Phoenix townsite.

The three-square block park is home to the **Arizona Doll and Toy Museum**, with antique toys from around the world and a reconstructed 19th-century schoolroom. Allow at least an hour to enjoy the museum fully. Open Tue-Sat 10am-4pm and Sun noon-4pm (phone 602-262-5071).

North Mountain Park offers almost 300 acres of mountain and desert, plus nature trails and a ranger on duty from sunrise to 10pm (10600 N. 7th St., phone 602-495-0981).

The **Phoenix Art Museum,** at 1625 N. Central Ave. (phone 602-257-1222), displays art from the Medieval, Renaissance, and French Baroque periods, plus Western and Far Eastern art. In October and November each year, the museum holds its acclaimed Cowboy Artists of America exhibition. Free only on Wednesdays, when it's open 5pm-9pm (guided tour at 6pm).

The **Pueblo Grande Museum and Cultural Park** depicts the ancient Hohokam Indian civilization with village ruins, irrigation canals, and a prehistoric ball court. The museum auxiliary holds an Indian Market in December each year showcasing the crafts of hundreds of tribes. The museum, located at 4619 E. Washington St. (phone 602-495-0900), is open Mon-Sat 9am-4pm and Sun 1pm-4pm (closed major holidays).

South Mountain Park covers 17,000 acres and is filled with rock formations, peaks, and canyons. Trees and cactus native to Arizona are marked for identification, and lookout points offer spectacular views of the city. The park is eight miles south of town on S. Central Ave. (phone 602-495-0222); open daily 6am-11:30pm.

The latest development in downtown Phoenix is **Hance Deck Park**, a 29-acre green belt stretching from 3rd St. to 3rd Ave. A paved plaza with fountains, a wooded area of elms, and a park with a volleyball court and picnic ramadas are open to the public. Plans call for a reflecting pool, a reconstructed Irish farmhouse, and a Japanese garden that will symbolize the city's ties to Hemeji, Japan.

Adjacent to the Phoenix Civic Plaza is **The Mercado**, with colorful buildings, brick-lined streets, and musical performances in a lively atmosphere of Mexican culture.

Nearby **Scottsdale**, whose streets have Western storefronts and where autos must yield to horses, recalls the Old West each February with the **Parada del Sol**, complete with horse-drawn floats, "shootouts" on Main Street, street dances, and Pony Express mail delivery to the Post Office. A month of special events includes dances, chili cook-offs, and Indian pow-wows, all leading up to the parade. The parade's free; there's an admission charge for the rodeo that follows. From late January to mid-March, the **Scottsdale Celebration of Fine Arts** features over 100 artists who work in all media.

Maps with self-guiding tours of Scottsdale are available at the Chamber of Commerce, 7343 Scottsdale Mall (phone 602-945-8481). On the mall, there's a park and the **Center for the Arts**, with changing exhibits of visual and performing arts, all free. It's open Mon-Sat 10am-5pm, Sun noon-5pm (phone 602-994-2301).

The **Fleischer Museum**, 17207 N. Perimeter Dr. in Scottsdale, contains some 200 American paintings from 1900-1940. Cameras are not allowed. Open daily 10am-4pm, closed on holidays (phone 602-585-3108).

In March, there's an **Arts Festival** with free concerts, children's art, and works by local and traveling artists, and on Sundays in April, Central Avenue is closed to traffic for the **Sunday on Central** celebration with fun for everyone. Parades, arts, food, and entertainment take over the neighborhood between McDowell and Osborne Roads from 11am-4pm (phone 602-256-0026). A **free concert and tree-lighting ceremony** is held annually in December on the Scottsdale Mall.

Mesa is in the Valley of the Sun on a plateau overlooking Phoenix. Founded by Indians, it was soon settled by the Mormons, who still use portions of the Indians' old irrigation canals. The **Arizona Temple Visitor Center**, at 525 E. Main St., features a program on the history of the Mormon religion. Guided 30-minute tours are given each day on the half-hour. During Easter Week, the Temple performs a **Passion Play**, and all through December the center is ablaze with Christmas lights. Open daily 9am-9pm (phone 602-964-7164).

Just south of town off I-10 on Wintersburg Rd., the **Palo Verde Nuclear Generating Station** offers narrated bus tours by reservation. The Energy Information Center displays various energy sources. Open Mon-Fri 8am-3pm and on Saturday if you make an appointment (phone 602-393-5757).

Chandler, another suburb of Phoenix, has an unusual celebration each March—the **Ostrich Festival**. There are exhibits, live music, Hispanic and Irish entertainment, an international food bazaar, a carnival, and a parade, but the big event is the ostrich races. The birds can't fly, but they sure can run! Phone 602-963-4571 for dates and times. Chandler also hosts an annual **Tumbleweed Christmas Tree Lighting Ceremony** with a parade of lights at 6pm and food and crafts vendors. It's at A.J. Park in downtown Chandler (phone 602-963-4571).

Tempe, also a suburb of Phoenix, holds its **Spring Festival of the Arts** in March, when the streets come alive with pedestrians and performers. This annual event showcases the crafts of local artists (phone 602-967-4877).

Back in Phoenix in November, you can see a hot air balloon race at the **Thunderbird Balloon Classic**. Balloon racers from around the world compete for prizes at the two-day event. Phone 602-978-7208 for dates and times.

Christmas is a magical time of year in the desert. The indoor concourse of the downtown Bank One Center at 201 N. Central in Phoenix is open daily from 8am-9pm for an **International Christmas Display** featuring ethnic dolls and a forest of trees decorated with an international flair. Call 602-221-1005 for information about special events such as concerts and things for the kids to do.

Fountain Hills, a planned community between Scottsdale and Mesa, is home to the **world's highest fountain**. Every hour on the hour, the fountain shoots a geyser of water 560 feet high for 15 minutes. The fountain is located in a 28-acre lake off Saguaro Blvd. The park is open from dawn-11pm daily, and the fountain erupts from 10am-9pm.

The Phoenix and Valley of the Sun Visitors Bureau has a map of the city and surrounding suburbs and a booklet on current events (One Arizona Center, 400 Van Buren St., Suite 600, Phoenix, AZ 85004; phone 602-254-6500).

PRESCOTT

If you woke suddenly and found yourself in an old Victorian town, you'd probably never guess you were in Arizona. Prescott, founded in 1864, is one of the prettiest, most charming towns in the Southwest. Surrounded by over a million acres of preserved national forests, the village was first settled by gold prospectors and is now filled with Victorian homes and historic buildings. A brochure describing a self-guided tour of the town is available at the Chamber of Commerce, 117 W. Goodwin St. (phone 520-445-2000 or 800-266-7534).

The unusual **Bead Museum,** at 140 S. Montezuma St., displays beads from all parts of the world, along with changing exhibits on personal adornments. Beads have been used as currency, as religious items, and also to teach geographic history and art. The museum is open 9:30am-4:30pm Mon-Sat, closed on major holidays (phone 520-445-2431).

Prescott's three-acre **Sharlot Hall Museum** is a wonderful collection of old homes, the Governor's Mansion (which has been reconstructed on the original site), a blacksmith house, the first house built in Prescott ("Old Fort Misery"), and a rose garden. Along with pioneer artifacts, you'll find prehistoric Southwestern Indian pieces. Open April-Oct 10am-5pm Tue-Sat and Nov-March 10am-4pm Tue-Sat. Sunday hours are 1pm-5pm (phone 520-445-3122).

The scenery surrounding Prescott is breathtaking. **Granite Basin** is a ten-acre lake just 12 miles northwest of town, and **Granite Dells**, only four miles north on SR 89, is a popular summer retreat on Watson Lake. The highway is ridged with massive granite formations, great for photos.

Prescott's **Frontier Days** celebration, held the first week in July, dates to 1888 and abounds with parades and entertainment of all kinds. Prescott is known throughout the Southwest for its Christmas season lighting of the Victorian homes in town. The ceremony at the courthouse is followed by an exquisitely lighted parade. In May, there's a **Mountain Artist Guild Art and Craft Show** on the Courthouse Plaza under the trees, followed by a street fair later in the month. June brings the **Inter-Tribal All-Indian Powwow**, and August offers the **Native American Festival and Powwow** at Watson Lake.

QUARTZSITE

Originally built to protect settlers from the Mojave Indians, Quartzsite was later a stagecoach stop on the way to Prescott. Today the town is home to the world's largest gem and mineral show, **The Main Event**.

Most of the year, Quartzsite is a sleepy desert town of about 2,000, but in late January something happens that's hard to believe unless you've seen it for yourself. The population of Quartzsite swells to *one million people* during the mineral show. The eight major shows are supplemented by smaller shows set up all over town. Thousands of dealers display rocks, gems, and minerals. The two-week event opens with a five-day powwow and includes hot-air balloons, rodeos, potluck suppers, fireworks, camel and ostrich races, antique vehicles, country-western dances, desert bonfires, and lots more. And everything is free! The show is also billed as "the largest gathering of RV'ers in the world." People come in droves, parking their RV's anywhere they can find a vacant space.

One of the most-visited places in town is the final resting place of **Hadji Ali**, better known as "Hi Jolly." He came to Arizona in the 1850's with a large number of camels ordered by the U.S. Army. The camels, with their nasty dispositions, didn't get along with the army mules and were soon discarded. Ali kept some for himself and tried to run a freight operation, but it was not successful. Eventually, the camels were set free, and Ali settled in Quartzsite as a prospector until his death in 1902. **Hi Jolly Daze**, a celebration complete with parades, a barbecue, and a dance, is held on the Saturday before Thanksgiving to honor the camel driver and welcome back all the "snowbirds" who winter here.

A rock hunter's paradise surrounds Quartzsite. Agates and

quartz are good finds, but there are many different stones waiting to be discovered.

One of the best sights in the state is the **Kofa National Wildlife Refuge**, which preserves the habitat of the desert bighorn sheep. Twenty miles south of Quartzsite off Hwy. 95, it's one of the few places in Arizona where native palms grow. You reach the park via a steep — but rewarding — climb. The refuge and palm canyon are always open (phone 520-783-7861).

The Quartzsite Chamber of Commerce is at Box 85, Quartzsite, AZ 85346 (phone 520-927-5600).

SACATON

When the Spanish missionaries first came to Sacaton in 1696, the site was an ancient Pima Indian village. Today it's headquarters of the **Pima Indian Reservation**.

The **Gila Indian Center** next to I-10 on Casa Blanca Rd. is comprised of reconstructed villages depicting thousands of years of Indian life in the Southwest. Six different tribes are represented, and a museum and a crafts center adjoin the park. Allow at least two hours to see everything. It's open daily from 9am-5pm, closed on holidays (phone 520-963-3981).

SEDONA

Overlooking Oak Creek Canyon in the middle of Red Rock Country, Sedona is one of the most scenic places in the Southwest. The town is a center for artists and craftspeople; jewelers, weavers, clothing designers, and painters abound.

The magic of Sedona is the spirit world. According to a legend of The People, Grandmother Spirit of the World still lives in Sedona, welcoming her family home, and the area has attracted various tribes for centuries: the Anasazi, the Hopi, the Apache, and the Yavapai. The town, known internationally as a center for mystics and paranormal happenings, lures visitors from all over the world for inspiration and enlightenment. Many psychics, astrologers, and New Age healers live in Sedona and counsel residents and tourists year round.

For some of the best area scenery, take West Hwy. 89A to the **Upper Red Rock Loop Road**, one of the most photographed places in America. You can picnic here, but there's no overnight camping. The towering rocks of Sedona inspired the designers of the **Chapel of the Holy Cross**, about three miles south of the intersection of Highways 179 and 89A. A beautiful shrine built into the red cliffs, it's open daily 8:30am-6pm from April-Oct (9am-5pm the rest of the year).

Fishermen will want to visit the **Page Springs Fish Hatchery**, 12 miles south of town. It's open every day from 8am-4pm (phone 520-634-4805).

The grounds at **Tlaquepaque** offer a replica of a Spanish village, with fountains and flowers. It's well worth seeing.

The **Sedona Arts Center** on Art Barn Rd. presents visual and performing arts featuring local artists. Open Tue-Sat 10:30am-4:30pm and Sun 1:30pm-4:30pm; closed Dec. 25-Jan. 1 (phone 520-282-3809). Sedona offers art throughout the year, with outdoor concerts in the Red Rock area and nationally acclaimed art and sculpture events.

On **Easter morning**, services are held at dawn on Table Top Mountain, two miles west on Hwy. 89A.

The best part of Sedona is the **scenery**: sandstone cathedrals, pine forests, and stunning sunsets. Tours to the outlying canyons reveal ruins left by an earlier people; some still have blackened corn cobs in the fire pit. Visitors can explore these past settlements with journeys into the various rock canyons. Among those who tended the orchards and farmland along the banks of rippling Oak Creek was a lovely young maiden named Sedona. Today, the cool summer nights, the gold autumn leaves drifting down Oak Creek, the occasional frosting of snow on the majestic red rocks, and the colorful blooms of spring entice visitors from all over the world. Just strolling through the many galleries and shops in town fills a day.

The Chamber of Commerce is in the middle of town at Forest Rd. and Hwy 89A (phone 520-282-7722 or 800-288-7336).

THATCHER

Settled by the Mormons in 1881, Thatcher is home to **The Museum of Anthropology** at Eastern Arizona State College, featuring collections from excavations in the Southwest, including an exhibition of pre-Columbian artifacts. It's open Mon-Fri 9am-noon and 1pm-4pm from late August to May (phone 520-428-8310).

TOMBSTONE

Known as "The Town Too Tough to Die," Tombstone, the best-known of the original mining camps, was named after a prospector who was told he'd find only his tombstone and no silver. He surprised everyone with a claim, which he named Tombstone, and rumors of riches made a boomtown of the settlement. During the next seven years, the mines yielded millions in silver and gold.

Of course, the town is most famous for the shootout at the **O.K. Corral** between the Earps and the Clantons. The corral is on Allen St. (one block off the highway, but really the main street of town), and the shootout is recreated in May each year during **Wyatt Earp Days**, and on the first and third Sunday of each month at 2pm (phone 520-457-3929).

A variety of free celebrations commemorate events of the 1880's. **Territorial Days** in March features an 1880's fashion parade, a pet parade, and fire-cart races. The **Revue of the Gunfighters** is held in September, and **Helldorado Days** come along in October; each has parades, chili contests, and mock gunfights on the main street. November hosts the more peaceful **Emmett Kelley Days**. The second generation of the famous clown's family lives in Tombstone, and the annual event includes a clown fashion show, face-painting, games, live entertainment, and a parade.

Board sidewalks and old-fashioned storefronts contribute to the atmosphere of the town, and many of the historic buildings are within a three-block area. Stroll around town and visit **St. Paul's Church** (built in 1882), the saloon called the **Crystal Palace**, and the **Tombstone Epitaph**, where the oldest newspaper in Arizona is still published. A history exhibit in the front office is free to the public.

Your last stop, appropriately, should be **Boot Hill Graveyard**, which contains marked graves of settlers, including desperados of old. The first cemetery in the West to be called Boot Hill, it's open daily 7:30am-6pm (phone 520-457-9344).

The Tombstone Chamber of Commerce address is P.O. Box 995, Tombstone, AZ 85638 (phone 520-457-3197).

TUBAC

Tubac is a town of firsts. The first European settlement in Arizona, it was also the site of the state's first schoolhouse, the first newspaper, the first Spanish land grant, and the first state park. According to archeologists, people have lived along the Santa Cruz River for at least 10,000 years. Five flags representing Tubac's past fly over the entrance to the town: Spain, Mexico, the Confederacy, Arizona, and the United States. Tubac was also the site of the first *presidio*, and ancient Tubac is still visible in the Presidio Museum, St. Ann's Church, the old schoolhouse, old adobe walls, and the state park.

Tubac today is an artist's haven, with an annual **Arts Festival** in February. Exhibits around town include watercolors, sculpture, and jewelry. In December, the **Intercultural Fiesta** at Tumacacori National Monument features food, arts, and entertainment, and the entire village is festooned with *luminarias*, the lighted Mexican decorations used throughout the Southwest. Also in December, *luminarias,* a large Christmas tree, and groups of carolers create a festive mood during the town's **Fiesta Navidad**. (A note of caution: when you walk the town to see the *luminarias,* bring a flashlight, since the glowing displays can create odd shadows on the walkways.) In May, a **Cinco de Mayo celebration** honors Mexico's special day. Art exhibits year-round celebrate the heritage that has made Tubac such a colorful town. And if you're not afraid of getting your hands dirty, a sanctioned **archeological dig** is underway, and tourists are invited to volunteer.

About three miles south of Tubac, the **Tumacacori National**

Historic Park encompasses the adobe ruins of a 17th century mission. At Christmastime, the mission has a display of 1,500 *luminarias* from 6-9pm (phone 520-398-2341 for details).

Hikers will enjoy the **Juan Bautista de Anza National Historic Trail** between Tubac and Tumacacori. The 4.5-mile trail runs beside the Santa Cruz River and follows a segment of the route taken by the Spanish explorer as he led colonists from Mexico to settle San Francisco.

The address of the Chamber of Commerce is P.O. Box 1866, Tubac, AZ 85646 (phone 520-398-2704).

TUCSON

Set in a long, green valley and encircled by four mountain ranges, Tucson has more sunny days a year than any other city in the U.S. The city is also the oldest continually inhabited settlement in the country, founded over 12,000 years ago by Indians who called the settlement *stjukshon* ("spring at the foot of the black hill"). In 1700, Spanish Jesuit priest Father Francisco Kino established San Xavier del Bac Mission to preach to the Indians, and soon ranchers and cattlemen followed. After the Apache attacked to protect their territory, a walled *presidio* was built in 1776 to protect the settlers; the city's nickname "The Old Pueblo" came from the walls. Today, adobe houses intermingle with high-rise buildings in the downtown area.

You'll feel Tucson's heritage — Spanish, Mexican and Indian — immediately. Indian dialects can be heard around town, and Spanish is widely spoken. Mt. Lemmon, which overlooks the city to the north, is the southernmost ski-able peak in the continental U.S. and a cool escape from the city's heat in the summer. Alpine chalets, groves of aspen and pine, and small lakes nestle in the ridges, surprising anyone who thinks the desert is all scrub and cactus. The summer also brings purple sunsets, rainbows, and skies so clear that stargazing is a favorite local pastime.

The **Arizona Historical Society Museum** is a library, museum, and mining exhibit near the entrance of the University of Arizona (open Mon-Sat 10am-4pm & Sun noon-4pm; phone

520-628-5774). Also on campus, the **Mineral Museum** displays gems, fossils, and minerals from around the world. It's open Mon-Fri 8am-3pm (phone 520-621-4227).

The **Arizona State Museum**, on the campus at Park and University, has displays about the archeology and ethnicity of the state. Its Southwest archeological collection is considered the most extensive in the world. You'll find exhibits on pottery-making and village life, and a presentation contrasting ancient and modern Indian life. Open Mon-Sat 10am-5pm and noon-5pm on Sun; closed on holidays (phone 520-621-6302).

The **Center for Creative Photography** houses one of the largest collections of photography in the world. Changing exhibits feature the world's foremost photographers; taped interviews and lectures are available upon request. The port-folios of dozens of major artists are on display, and over 50,000 photos can be seen in the print viewing room. The Center, on the University campus at 2nd St. just off Speedway, is open Mon-Fri 11am-5pm (phone 520-621-7968).

The **Flandreau Science Center and Planetarium**, also at the University on the main campus, offers exhibits of astronomy and space exploration. Its 16-inch telescope is available free for night viewing, and many of the exhibits are "hands on." Open Tue-Thur 9am-5pm and 7pm-9pm, and Friday and Saturday nights until midnight (phone 520-621-7827).

Yet another free attraction on the University campus is the **University Museum of Art**, one block east of Park near Speedway. Among the museum's large collection of 20th-century art are works by Picasso, Rodin, and Wyeth. Open Mon-Fri 9am-5pm from mid-August to mid-May (phone 520-621-7567).

The **DeGrazia Gallery in the Sun** displays the artist's multi-media work. The original architecture of the open-air chapel, the "Mission in the Sun," was also done by the artist. Open daily 10am-4pm; closed Easter, Christmas, and Thanksgiving Day (6300 N. Swan Road; phone 520-299-9191).

The **Fort Lowell Museum**, in Ft. Lowell Park at Ft. Lowell and Craycroft St., is in the ruins of the old fort and contains three rooms that have been reconstructed to their 1885 appearance. Photography and military exhibits are on display. Open Wed-Sat 10am-4pm (phone 520-885-3832). In February, free tours of the old Ft. Lowell neighborhood run during **La Reunión de El Fuerte**, a celebration exploring the heritage of this unique section of Tucson, from the Hohokam people to the Mormons, Mexicans, and American soldiers. The tours begin in the park. And in early April, the Fort's **Pioneer Days** re-create the handiwork, dance, food, and music of the 19th century. The Buffalo Soldiers Troop appears, and you can see a quilting bee, cake walk, and various historic displays. For details, call 520-297-5540.

Reid Park at 22nd and Country Club is a 160-acre park in the center of Tucson. There are picnic areas, a fishing lake, tennis courts, and a baseball field where the Colorado Rockies hold spring training and the Tucson Toros (Pacific Coast League) play their home games. Fishing is free for kids under 14; there's a $3.50 fee to go into the 17-acre zoo. The park is open daily 7am-10pm.

The **John C. Fremont House** at 151 S. Granada Ave. has been restored and is open to the public at no charge. Fremont was territorial governor and lived in the house in 1880. Period furnishings abound, and in December the house is decorated for a Territorial Christmas. Allow at least an hour to see everything. Open Wed-Sat 10am-4pm; closed holidays (phone 520-622-0956).

The **R.W. Webb Winery**, 14 miles east of the city off Hwy. 10 on a frontage road, offers guided tours explaining the process of wine-making. The tours are free, but if you want to taste there's a $1 charge per person. The winery is open 10am-5pm weekdays and noon-5pm Sun (phone 520-762-5777).

The **Mission San Xavier del Bac** is the only mission in the country still actively preaching to the Indians. The building, called "The White Dove of the Desert," exemplifies Spanish architecture. A small crafts center is on the grounds nearby, and the Indians make and sell "fry-bread" in stands near the entrance gate. The ceilings and walls of the mission, smoky from years of burning candles and incense, were recently

Mission San Xavier del Bac. (photo: Greg Edwards)

cleaned and restored. Taped 15-minute talks are given every hour. Native American celebrations begin on the evenings of Oct. 3 and Dec. 2, and the reenactment of the founding of the mission is held annually on the first Friday after Easter. The mission is open daily 9:30am-4pm (phone 520-294-2624).

Tohono Chul Park is an oasis in the foothills of north Tucson. Once privately owned, the land was donated to the city to preserve the natural desert environment. Paths wind through the park and around little creeks and fountains; birds and wildlife are everywhere; and all cactus and trees are identified. Exhibit buildings have changing displays on Southwestern customs and art, and there's a small restaurant with outdoor tables, a greenhouse, a bookstore, and a gift shop. Tohono Chul is a delightful escape from the hustle of the big city (7336 N. Paseo del Norte, near the corner of Oracle and Ina; open Mon-Sat 9:30am-5pm, Sun 1pm-5pm; phone 520-575-8468).

Tucson Mountain Park, eight miles west on Kinney and Speedway Blvd., contains 17,000 acres of mountain and desert land, including one of the largest areas of saguaro growth. The saguaro cactus grows only in Arizona and northern Mexico, and the huge, multi-limbed plants take 200 years to reach their full height. The park has hiking trails and picnic facilities.

La Casa Cordova, built in 1850, is one of Tuscon's oldest buildings and is filled with displays of the city's Hispanic heritage. It's open Tue-Sat 10am-4pm and Sun noon-4pm, and it's located in the **El Presidio Historic District** north of Alameda Street. This is Tuscon's original neighborhood, built in the 1770's. In the same neighborhood, a popular place to spend time is **Old Town Artisans** at 186 N. Meyer Ave. Within a one-block area, adobes that were built along the original *presidio* wall have been restored and grouped around a garden courtyard. Hundreds of regional and Latin American artists display their works here.

Fourth Avenue between 4th and 7th Sts. is another great place to explore. Everything from antiques to the very latest in Southwestern wear can be found, and in April the **Fourth Avenue Street Fair** is a major happening. Face-painters, musicians, jugglers, mariachis, and artists all contribute to the fun.

On Sunday evenings in the spring, the Tucson Pops Orchestra presents **Music Under the Stars** in Reid Park. And in **Udall Park** (Tanque Verde and Sabino Canyon Rds.), the Arizona Symphonic Winds present free concerts under the stars throughout the summer months. In April, the **Fiesta del Presidio** celebrates Tuscon's Hispanic heritage with two days of art and entertainment that include piñata-making, traditional Mexican dancing and food, and displays of rope-twirling, all held in downtown Presidio Park. Throughout the year, the first and third Saturday night of each month is designated **Downtown Saturday Night**. There are street dances and arts and crafts exhibits everywhere, along with musical groups and strangely costumed people. The area is especially beautiful at Christmas, when horse-drawn carriages make their way from downtown to Winterhaven, a neighborhood that decorates lavishly for the holiday.

The **Tanque Verde Greenhouses** at 10810 E. Tanque Verde is a good place to learn about desert vegetation. You'll be surprised to see over 600 species of cactus and succulents on this three-acre spread. There are desert display gardens, four greenhouses, and a showroom. It's open 9am-5pm Mon-Sat (phone 520-749-4414).

At the **Saguaro National Monument West**, 2700 N. Kinney Rd., the visitors center features exhibits of flora and fauna from the Sonoran Desert and a slide program called "Voices of the Desert," which describes the Indian relationship to the desert and the saguaro cactus (phone 520-733-5158).

Held in mid-December, the **Winterhaven Festival of Lights** celebrates Christmas in the neighborhood bounded by Ft. Lowell, Country Club and Prince Roads, and Tucson Blvd. There are walking tours and a special Sun Tran bus.

Each spring, Tucson hosts the **International Mariachi Conference**, with world-class bands, singers, and folk dancers. Some of the free events during the conference include a parade, the Fiesta at Armory Park, and the Mariachi mass at the convention center. Call 520-884-9920 for details.

A celebration of the music and culture of the Tohono O'Odham Indians is held in late April at the **Waila Festival**. The sounds of Bavaria, filtered through 200 years of Spanish history in Mexico, are mixed with tribal sounds to produce *waila*. For dates and times, contact the Arizona Historical Society at 949 E. 2nd St. (phone 520-628-5774).

A tradition that dates to 1775, **La Fiesta de San Augustine** is celebrated each August and honors Tucson's patron saint with a variety of free activities, including an evening street dance, at the Arizona Historical Society. Call 520-628-5774 for more.

The lovely **Garden of Gethsemane** is on W. Congress St., just a few blocks from downtown on the west bank of the Santa Cruz River. It's the work of local sculptor Felix Lucero.

Philabaum Glass Gallery and Studios, 711 S. 6th Ave., offer glass-blowing exhibitions, transforming molten glass into beautiful objects before your eyes. Call 520-884-7404 for demonstration times.

Finally, don't miss **Sabino Canyon**, open 8am-4:30pm daily (phone 520-749-3223). The Santa Catalina Mountains form a mammoth triangle cut by steep canyons; Sabino is the largest. Most of the year a cold, clear mountain stream runs through it, fed by the snow from the peaks above. The visitors center at the entrance has a series of exhibits explaining the geology and history of the area, and a marked trail leads to some of the finest views in the state. You can't take your car inside the park. (A shuttle tram costs $5.) Hikers will also find trails at Catalina State Park, the Rillito River Walk, and Madera Canyon. Bird-watchers will be happy in Tohono Chul, Ramsey Canyon, Sabino Canyon, and Agua Caliente Park.

The Tucson Visitors Bureau is located at 130 S. Scott Ave., Tucson, AZ 85701. Open Mon-Fri 8:30am-5pm, Sat & Sun 9am-4pm (phone 520-624-1817).

WICKENBURG

The Wickenburg Chamber of Commerce has developed a self-guided **walking tour** and produced a delightful, hand-drawn brochure called *A Historic Day Out Wickenburg Way*. There are 19 points of interest, including the Pastime Pool Hall and the Wisdom House, home of the village smithy, which dates to the 1860's. You'll also see the 200-year-old mesquite Jail Tree, where, from 1863 to 1890, outlaws were chained for lack of a better place.

The nationally known **Hassayampa River Preserve** supports one of Arizona's best (and last) Sonoran Desert stream-side habitats. The cottonwood forest is one of the rarest forests in the country. Tours with a staff naturalist last an hour and a half and give an excellent introduction to the preserve. There's a reference library, a bookstore, and a self-guiding trail around Palm Lake. Hassayampa is an Apache word meaning "river that runs upside down," alluding to the fact that the river occasionally runs underground. The preserve is located three miles southwest of town on Hwy. 60/89/93; a sign marks the turn-off near milepost 114. In the winter, the park is open Wed-Sun 8am-5pm; in the summer, 6am-noon (phone 520-684-2772).

While you're in the area, don't miss the Wishing Well and the fable of the Hassayampa. If you take a drink from the river, face north, and make a wish, legend says you'll never tell the truth again. It's on Hwy. 60 at the northwest end of the Hassayampa Bridge.

About 25 miles north of Wickenburg is the village of **Yarnell**. North of the main highway, the **Shrine of St. Joseph of the Mountains** offers an open-air shrine with statues following the Stations of the Cross created in the natural granite boulders of the area. Always open.

One of several great hikes out of the Wickenburg area will take you to the **Wickenburg Inn**, situated in a wildlife preserve with a Desert Nature Center and a full-time naturalist. The **Box Canyon** on the Hassayampa River makes a good place for photography and picnics. **Vulture Peak**, named for the famous Vulture Mine, is part of the Vulture Mountains, a vast volcanic plateau. The hike is especially beautiful in the spring, when the desert is in full bloom.

WILLCOX

Willcox was the stronghold of the Chiricahua Apaches in the early 16th century. In 1886, after years of bloodshed between the Apaches and the soldiers at Ft. Bowie, the Indians were exiled to forts in Alabama, Florida, and Oklahoma. When the legendary Chief Cochise died in 1872, he was buried in the mountains nearby, along with his horse, dog, and rifle. Some say you can feel a presence in the mountains, perhaps the spirit of the great chief.

Southeast of the city, historic **Fort Bowie** was built in 1862 to guard the Butterfield Overland Stage Trail. You can reach the site only by hiking the last rugged mile and a half. Everything at the site is protected; digging tools, metal detectors, and guns are prohibited.

The **Cochise Visitor Center** (Exit 340 off Hwy. 10) houses Apache artifacts, including pottery shards, spear points, and an exhibit showing typical Indian living conditions. Military history displays feature cavalry weapons of the 1880's and a horse-drawn carriage. A striking bust of Chief Cochise is displayed, along with some of his sayings. The center is open Mon-Sat 9am-5pm, Sun 1pm-5pm (phone 520-384-2272).

The Chamber of Commerce in Willcox has created a brochure with a **walking tour** of the historic downtown area, including the **Schwertner House**, built in 1881 entirely of redwood and later used as a rooming house for Army personnel.

The newest winery in the state is in Willcox. **Kokopelli Winery** at 961 Haskell Ave. features zinfandel and Gewurztraminer and is open daily for tastings.

Annual town events include a **National Historic Preservation Week** in May with home tours, a territorial costume contest, antique show, and art exhibit. In October, Willcox celebrates **Rex Allen Days** to honor the hometown cowboy movie star. There are always parades, a rodeo, country music, and a cowboy dance as part of the fun. And in January, the **Wings over Willcox Sandhill Crane Celebration** salutes the hundreds of cranes that winter in the area. There are seminars, bird-watching tours, and children's activities. Call 520-384-2272 for more details.

Willcox is the center of apple country in Arizona, and each year around Christmas, there's an **Apple Festival** at the community center, with an arts and crafts show, a cooking-with-apples contest, a fashion show, and local entertainment, all free. It's sponsored by the Chamber of Commerce (phone 520-384-2272 or 800-200-2272).

WINDOW ROCK

Headquarters of the Navajo nation, Window Rock hosts the **Navajo Nation Fair** in early September at the fairgrounds with a parade, powwow, craft show, and traditional Indian dances and songs. Remember tribal restrictions — in addition to those already mentioned, cameras aren't allowed in some areas, so ask before you take a picture.

The **Navajo Tribal Museum** in the Arts and Crafts Building on SR 264 displays objects concerning the history and culture of the Navajo. Prehistoric tribal cultures are also explored, and you can investigate a re-created trading post of the 1800's. Allow at least an hour for this fascinating museum. It's open Mon-Sat 8am-6pm April-Sept; Mon-Fri 9am-6pm the rest of the year; closed on holidays (phone 520-871-6673).

St. Michael's Historical Museum contains permanent displays on the work of Franciscan Friars in the Navajo nation, with examples of Navajo culture and daily life. The museum, located in the original Franciscan mission building exhibited as it was in 1898, is off SR 264 about three miles. Open Mon-Sat 9am-5pm and Sun 10am-6pm from May 31st to the first week in Sept. (phone 520-871-4171).

YUMA

The California Gold Rush of 1849 lured thousands through the Yuma Crossing at Fort Yuma, one of Arizona's oldest military posts and the gateway to California. Yuma sits on the edge of the Colorado River; cross the bridge and you're in California. The city has a fascinating past — Spaniards visited the Quechan Indians at Yuma Crossing 80 years before the Pilgrims landed at Plymouth Rock—and many historic sites.

Fort Yuma, built in 1849, has been turned into the **Quechan Indian Museum** by the tribe. The fort overlooks the Colorado River, and the museum was the kitchen of the commanding officer when the military was in charge in the early 1850's. The walls have been restored to their original condition, and the museum contains displays of the Quechan Indian culture and its relation to the military in the 1800's, as well as the history of the early Spanish explorers. Open Mon-Fri 7am-noon and 1pm-4pm; closed holidays (phone 619-572-0661).

The **Arizona Historical Society Century House and Garden** at Fort Yuma is one of Yuma's oldest, most historic buildings. Displays on Indian culture, photographs, and furnishings of the territorial period fill the house. Outside, you can tour beautiful gardens and aviaries with exotic and talking birds. Open Tue-Sat 10am-4pm all year (phone 520-782-1841). The **St. Thomas Mission** is also on the grounds at the fort.

On the banks of the Colorado behind City Hall on 2nd Street sits Southern Pacific steam engine #2521. Built in 1907, it saw almost 3,000,000 miles of service before being retired in 1957. The kids will love seeing the old engine and sitting in the engineer's seat.

Several old ghost towns are near Yuma. **Gold Rock Ranch** is 29 miles northwest off I-8, and nearby **Tumco** once yielded $11,000,000 in gold. The ruins of the adobe home of one of Yuma's pioneers is east on Hwy. 95.

The **Neely Tompkins Gallery** and the **Colorado River Pottery** are both working studios on Second St., open to visitors. The **Yuma Art Center**, located in the old Southern Pacific Depot on Gila St., is a visual arts center and museum open Tue-Sat year-round from 10am-5pm.

Theater buffs will enjoy seeing the **Yuma Theatre**, originally opened in 1911 as an opera house with an orchestra pit and proscenium stage. The theater, restored and popular again, is the only theater in Arizona with an organ. The Cultural Council will be happy to give tours for interested groups (phone 520-783-2423).

The Peanut Patch Farm is located on the Didier family farm on the original homestead at 4322 E. County 13th St. During peanut harvest (Oct-Dec), tours are conducted through the shelling plant. The farm grows, harvests, roasts, processes, and packages peanuts, as well as citrus, dates, and dried fruit. The aroma alone makes a tour worthwhile. It's open daily 9am-6pm (phone 520-726-6292).

The annual **Southwest Indian Powwow Dances** are usually held the first week in March. The ceremonial dress and dances date back hundreds of years and vividly portray the beautiful customs of the tribes from the mountain and coastal areas of the country.

The **Imperial National Wildlife Refuge** covers almost 26,000 acres along the Colorado River. The Arizona section is off US 95, about 40 miles north of Yuma; the rest of the refuge can be reached only by boat. Hiking, hunting, and fishing are permitted in designated areas. Maps are available on request. Open daily from dawn to dusk year-round. For information, contact the Refuge Manager, Imperial National Wildlife Refuge, Box 72217, Yuma, AZ 85365 (phone 520-783-3371).

Detailed maps of Yuma and lots of free brochures are available from the Convention and Visitors Bureau, 488 S. Maiden Ln., Yuma, AZ 85364 (phone 520-783-0071).

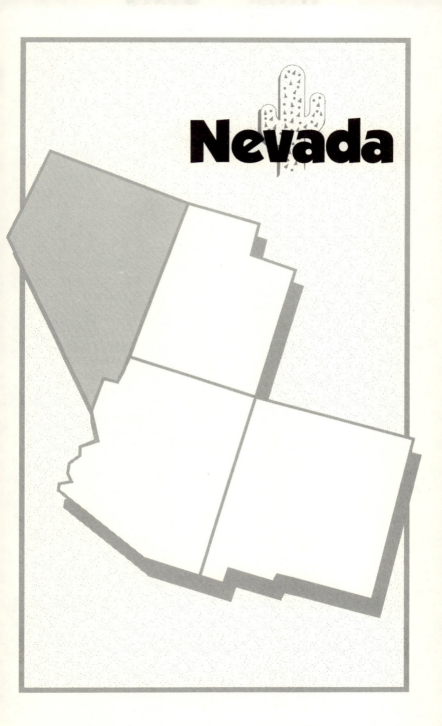

Nevada

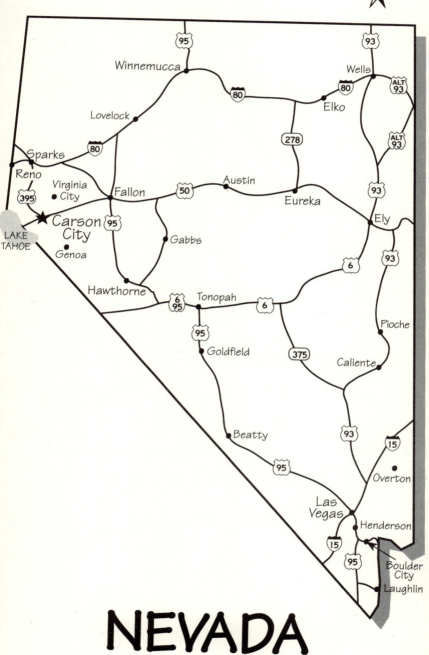

NEVADA

Nevada

When they visit Nevada, most people think only of gambling and returning home with a small fortune. Those same people also think that Nevada, with its glitzy cities and celebrity-filled nightclubs, will cost a small fortune to visit.

They're wrong on both counts. Few gamblers hit the jackpot — after all, how do you think casinos pay their electric bills? — and Nevada has innumerable inexpensive and free attractions.

There are two sides to Nevada. One is a snazzy picture of glamorous entertainment, neon, gourmet dining, and first-class hotels. The other is a timeless land with magnificent mountain ranges, lush valleys, and beautifully sparse deserts. The most mountainous of the 50 states, Nevada is an outdoor enthusiast's paradise, with lakes set like sapphires in the desert, wind whistling through ancient bristlecone pines, and sun glinting off centuries-old glacial ice. Despite the crush of people and traffic on Las Vegas's Strip, Nevada is a land where cows far outnumber cars, and it's not unusual to spot a cowboy herding cattle or a hawk skimming across the sky in search of a jackrabbit.

Nevada lies almost entirely within the Great Basin, with several rocky peaks topping 10,000 feet. Millions of acres are protected by the federal government and managed by the U. S. Forest Service; only those on foot or horsebackare allowed on these lands.

With its vast deserts, Nevada was a terrifying obstacle to those in wagon trains heading for California. The first permanent settlement of whites in the state was Mormon Station, now called Genoa, a trading post established in what is now Carson Valley at the foot of the Sierra Nevadas. The region drew treasure-seekers, however, when silver was discovered at Virginia City in the 1850's. The Comstock Lode, one of the richest bodies of ore ever found, turned Nevada into a major destination — and a desirable addition to the United States. (Nevada became a state in 1864.) The silver boom in Virginia City created millionaires who built lavish mansions in the town and the nearby Washoe Valley. Many of their homes still stand and are open to visitors.

When the silver ran out, Nevada fell into a depression, but it lasted only a few years. Gold was discovered in Tonopah and Goldfield around 1900, and miners found copper at Ely. Mining remains an important industry in Nevada. Silver and turquoise are still dug, and a gold mine — now the world's largest — opened in 1965 near Elko.

Shepherds from the Basque region of Spain came to Nevada to raise sheep, and irrigation brought farms in the valleys and livestock on acres of open range. Today, you can attend a Basque festival, enjoy the dusty fun of a camel race, or listen to a cowboy read his poetry at the Cowboy Poetry Gathering. The National Wildlife Refuge at Pahranagat is a favorite spot for duck hunting; elk and deer are plentiful northwest of Las Vegas. Lake Tahoe, the largest alpine lake in North America, boasts more ski resorts than anywhere in the country, and the snow stays well into spring. The lake also has sandy beaches, campgrounds, and terrific fishing spots. Hot springs bubble out of the desert floor, and icy streams run beside hiking trails.

Southern Nevada is a treasure trove for rock hunters; turquoise, fire opals, jasper, agate, and crystals are easy to find. You might like to visit a chocolate and marshmallow factory in Henderson or gaze at the fiery red sandstone formations in the

Valley of Fire near Las Vegas. Back in civilization, the oldest bar in Nevada still operates in Genoa, and Winnemucca offers a taste of the Pyrenees with its Basque festivals.

For a memorable drive, take Highway 50, which follows the old Pony Express trail, where traces of long-ago stations are still visible. When *Life* magazine named the highway "the loneliest road in America" and said it had no attractions and no points of interest, the folks living along the road responded with a "survival kit" that includes a map that can be validated in towns along the way. Nevadans know that Highway 50 is in fact one of the most scenic drives in the West. The road passes through wide valleys and past mountain ranges that seem to stretch forever.

Gambling, legalized in Nevada in 1931, is the main source of revenue for the state. And thanks to the casinos, which compete fiercely for patrons, Nevada is an inexpensive place to visit. Food, lodging, and entertainment are a bargain, and most of the larger casinos offer free attractions. (Well, they're free as long as you can resist putting cash into a slot machine.)

AUSTIN

Austin is a ghost of its former self, but it's not a ghost town. In the 1800's, the town had a population over 10,000; today, it's about 400.

All western towns seem to have one bizarre, whimsical residence. In Austin, **Stoke's Castle**, a deserted three-story replica of a Roman tower, was built of hand-hewn granite in 1897 by Anson Stokes, who made his fortune from silver found nearby. The structure, situated to provide a spectacular view of the valley, can be seen for miles, rising from the desert floor.

Austin's **Catholic Church** is the oldest in the state, and the **Methodist Church**, in use since 1866, was financed by the pastor with money raised from mining stocks.

Near Austin, the **Hickson Petroglyph Recreation Site** features Indian carvings on stone from 1000 B.C. The site is 24 miles east of town off US 50. West of town off SR 50 are the remains of the **Pony Express Station** at Cold Springs. Highway signs explain the history and mark the beginning of a 1.5-mile trail leading to the station.

Between Austin and Fallon at **Grimes Point Archeological Site**, interpretive signs point the way along a trail lined with boulders covered with petroglyphs made by those who lived in the area between 5000 B.C. and 1500 A.D.

BEATTY

Beatty is the entrance to **Death Valley National Monument**, which protects an area formed about three million years ago. Also on the same road, SR 374, are the ghost towns of **Rhyolite** and **Bullfrog**. Rhyolite is one of the best and most accessible ghost towns in the Southwest. Only stone foundations and brick storefronts remain in a town that once had an opera house, telephones, saloons, hundreds of homes, schools, and three railroads. The train depot and a house constructed entirely of glass bottles still stand. Be careful when visiting any ghost town; the structures are very old and worn and can be dangerous to explore.

Nearby Death Valley is a land of contrasts. Shifting desert sands meet snowcapped mountains, and spring-fed oases co-exist with borax flats. Within the valley you can see the **Harmony Borax Works**, historic home of the 20-mule-team borax wagons. The site is open weekdays from 9am-4pm.

In March, Rhyolite holds an annual festival featuring living-history tours and exhibits, old movies, and a historical drama. Call 702-553-2424 for details.

Beatty's small Chamber of Commerce can be reached at Box 956, Beatty, NV 89003 (phone 702-553-2225).

BOULDER CITY

Built in the 1930's, Boulder City was created to house the federal employees who constructed Hoover Dam and is the gateway to Lake Mead National Recreation Area. The town is still the only place in Nevada without legalized gambling. A historic district **walking tour** along covered walkways highlights the company houses and the old **Boulder City Hotel**, a registered landmark and historic resort preserved with elegance and charm. The **Burk Gallery** features local and national artists exhibiting original art in oils, watercolors, and bronzes.

A **Spring Jamboree** is held each April, and in July there's a celebration called **Damboree**, with parades, costume contests, and cook-offs. October brings **Art in the Park**, a show featuring Western artists and crafts, and in December the **Christmas Parade** lights up the town.

Hoover Dam, one of the highest dams ever constructed, is considered one of the engineering marvels of the U.S. Movies about the construction are shown in a theater near the Nevada Spillway. Free shuttle service from parking lots along US 93 is provided during dam tour hours. Elevators carry visitors down to the power plant for a 40-minute guided tour every day from 8am-6pm from May 31-Labor Day. The rest of the year, the tours run from 9am-4pm. The last tour leaves an hour before closing. The Exhibit Building at the west end of the dam displays a model of the entire river basin, along with a taped lecture. The building is open daily 8am-6pm May 31-Labor Day (9am-4pm the rest of the year). The dam is closed on Christmas Day. For more information, call 702-293-8321.

Hoover Dam created **Lake Mead**, the largest manmade lake in the Western hemisphere: 115 miles long with a shoreline of 550 miles and countless water sports and outdoor activities.

Alan Bible was a long-time and much-loved Senator from Nevada. At the **Alan Bible Visitor Center**, east of Boulder City on US 93, you'll find an exhibit of natural history, films, and all kinds of information about the lake. The center, in the middle of botanical gardens featuring desert plants and flowers, is open daily 8:30am-4:30pm (closed major holidays). You can fish and swim in the lake all year; a fishing license is necessary. In December, don't miss Lake Mead's **Parade of Lights**.

CALIENTE

Visitors to Caliente will find a quiet railroad town known for its Spanish-mission style **railroad depot**, which rises above every building in the village. A mural with nearby points of interest

Hoover Dam and Lake Mead. (photo: E.E. Hertzog)

decorates the lobby, and guided tours of the **Lincoln County Art Room** can be arranged through the Chamber (phone 702-726-3129).

On Memorial Day weekend, Caliente hosts the **Lincoln County Homecoming**, with arts shows, a parade, and a rodeo.

CARSON CITY

The best way to see Carson City, Nevada's capital since territorial days, is on foot. A free map describing the **Historic Mansion Walking Tour** is available from the Chamber of Commerce at 1900 S. Carson St., Suite 100 (phone 702-882-1565). Included on the tour is the colonial **Governor's Mansion**, built in 1908 and decorated for the first families who lived there. Visitors enter through a marble portico and tour state rooms, family rooms, parlors, and salons.

Perhaps the world's rarest collection of natural gold formations is on display at the **Carson City Nugget**. Valued at over a million dollars, the collection took nearly 70 years to accumulate. Gold sometimes assumes rare forms in the quartz veins in which it's found, and included in the collection are ribbon gold, wire gold, and crystallized gold. The Nugget, always open, is at 507 N. Carson St. (phone 702-882-1626).

The silver-domed **Nevada State Capitol** is a museum of the state's political history, and visitors are free to roam the native sandstone building with its hallways of polished Alaskan marble. Portraits of Nevada governors line the halls, and you can tour the Old Assembly and Senate chambers upstairs. Self-guiding tours are available Mon-Fri 8am-5pm (phone 702-687-3810). You can see lawmakers in action at the new **Legislative Building** south of the Capitol (open Mon-Fri 9am-4pm).

Antique firefighting equipment and a series of Currier and Ives prints dealing with firefighters are on display at the **Warren Engine Company No. 1 Fire Museum** at 777 S. Stewart St. It's open Mon-Fri 1pm-5pm (phone 702-887-2210).

The **Nevada State Railroad Museum** at 2180 S. Carson has a collection of restored Virginia and Truckee Railroad equipment. The line was used to haul ore from the Comstock Lode. On weekends from Memorial Day to Labor Day, the railroad offers rides for $2.50; the museum and grounds are free.

The **Stewart Indian Museum** at 5366 Snyder Ave. (phone 702-882-1808) is located on the campus of the old Stewart Indian Boarding School, listed in the National Register of Historic Places. Changing exhibits feature baskets, jewelry, pottery, and E.S. Curtis photogravures. Open daily 9am-4pm. In March and June, the museum hosts powwows that bring Native Americans from all over. Traditional and fancy dancers compete for awards; gaming, dancing, eating, and trading are all part of a powwow. Crafts shown include buckskin moccasins, handmade jewelry, and weavings.

Bowers Mansion State Park, 10 miles north of town on Old Hwy. 395, is a restored mansion built by a Virginia City millionaire for his wife in the 1800's. Some of the original furnishings were brought around Cape Horn by ship. The grounds, which overlook Washoe Lake, have picnic facilities, gardens, and a swimming pool. Tours of the mansion cost $3, but you can tour the grounds for free (phone 702-849-1825).

Carson City celebrates its place along the Pony Express Trail in June, with a **Kit Carson Rendezvous and Wagon Train Ride** re-enacting the ride from Sacramento, California to St. Joseph, Missouri. Between April 3, 1860 and Oct 18, 1861, dozens of brave young men carried mail by horseback across 1,800 miles and eight states, all the time facing danger from the elements, robbers, and hostile Indian tribes. The requirements for the riders were that they be "young skinny fellows not over 18. Must be expert riders willing to risk death daily. Orphans preferred." Four days after the completion of the first transcontinental telegraph line, the Pony Express went out of business.

ELKO

Lowell Thomas once called Elko the "last authentic cowtown in America." It's true. You'll still find genuine cowboys in Elko. Most of the time you'll have to head out to the range to see them, but during the last week of January, the renowned **Cow-**

boy Poetry Gathering takes place, and cowboys are everywhere. The event has grown from an informal get-together for a few dozen men into an international event that attracts thousands. Strange as it may seem, cowboys have a long tradition of reciting poetry. In addition to the literature, cowboys display skills such as silversmithing, leather work, and horsehair braiding. Poetry and music workshops run during the day, and there are readings and music performances at night. The workshops are free; there's a small charge for the performances. Recently, a **Cowboy Music Festival** was added, in late June, with the historic Pioneer Hotel as headquarters. Call 702-738-7508 or 888-880-5885 for information on dates and times.

Elko has a large Basque population, and the town celebrates that heritage annually with the **National Basque Festival** on the weekend nearest the fourth of July. During the colorful event, you get a view of Basque culture, customs, and personality. The fun begins with a parade and is followed by a day of contests like wood-chopping, sheep-herding, strength competitions, and a sheepdog exhibition. Parades, centuries-old folk dancing, and a talent show are all part of the fun.

The acclaimed **Northwest Nevada Museum**, one of the best museums in the state, contains displays on the lifestyle of the cowboys, the Basques, the Emigrant Trail, and indigenous wildlife. An 1860's Pony Express cabin is on the grounds, with a stagecoach and antique autos parked outside. Changing art exhibits are also featured. The museum, at 1515 Idaho St., is open Mon-Sat 9am-5pm, Sun 1pm-5pm (phone 702-738-3418).

Elko is a natural hub for side trips to ghost towns and the wilderness areas in the nearby **Ruby Mountains**, known as the Alps of Nevada, a wonderland of icy lakes and uncrowded hiking trails. **Lamoille Canyon** is famous for its steep, glacial walls. A 12-mile paved road, designated a National Scenic Highway, winds through the canyon and has signs along the way describing the canyon's natural wonders and the effects of glacial activity. Picnicking is permitted, and campgrounds are open in the summer.

Northeast of Elko on SR 226 is the historic mining town of **Tuscarora**. Points of interest include the cemetery, an open-pit mine, old buildings, a small museum, and a pottery school and gallery.

The **Jarbridge Wilderness Area** covers hundreds of acres of unspoiled alpine terrain. Fishing, hunting, and camping are allowed there on a first-come, first-served basis.

Jarbridge is the most inaccessible ghost town in Nevada, but it's worth the trip for those who want to walk in the past and listen for the ghostly shouts of miners long gone. The community is known as much for its spectacular setting as its historic ruins. Jarbridge was the site of the last stagecoach robbery in the U.S., in 1916. You'll find a saloon, an old jail, and several houses. From Elko, take the Mountain City Highway and then a dirt road accessible only in the summer. It's a great day trip from Elko.

The Elko Chamber of Commerce is at 1601 Idaho St., Elko, NV 89801 (phone 702-738-7135).

ELY

Ely is eastern Nevada's largest community, founded in 1868 as a silver mining camp. Several old mining camps and ghost towns remain in the area.

Ely's **White Pine Public Museum** has a collection of over 700 dolls, as well as Pony Express memorabilia, gems and minerals, and Indian relics. An outdoor exhibit includes steam engines from the early 1900's and several coaches. The address is 2000 Aultman St., and it's open Mon-Fri 8:30am-4pm, Sat & Sun 10am-4pm (phone 702-289-4710).

The **Ward Charcoal Ovens Historical Monument** is 12 miles south of Ely and reached by a graded gravel road off Hwy. 63. Built in the early 1870's to convert wood into charcoal for the mining operations at the old town of Ward, the ovens are 30 feet high and 27 feet around at the base. A small hole in the top provided ventilation, and each oven was capable of holding 35 cords of wood. In 1883, a fire destroyed most of the town, and today all that remains is a cemetery, the mill foundations, and the ovens. The monument is open all year, but it's more easily accessible during the summer.

Ely is the gateway to the **Great Basin National Park**, once described as "an island in the sky." The 78,000-acre park rises abruptly from the desert floor and contains stunning mountain peaks, meadows that burst with color in the spring, sparkling streams, and a small permanent ice field. Like all of Nevada's mountains, the range runs north to south in a curious pattern described by one geologist as resembling caterpillars marching towards Mexico. The wildlife includes mountain lions, mule deer, and golden eagles. Fishing for rainbow trout is popular, and hiking trails lead past pristine lakes to the 13,063-foot summit of Wheeler Peak, where the snow pack is unchanging and the view goes on forever.

The park is also home to the **Bristlecone Pine Forest**, 150 acres of trees said to be the oldest living things on earth. One stand has pines over 4,000 years old. Like the face of an old cowboy, the gnarled, twisted trees evoke character and dignity. Park interpreters lead walks through the forest every day from early June through early September.

The **Lexington Arch** is located near the southeast border of the park. An unpaved road leads to a trail head, from which you can hike to the picturesque limestone arch, more than six stories high.

You should carry drinking water when visiting the park, and remember that rattlesnakes are found at the lower elevations during warm weather. A 12-mile **Wheeler Peak Scenic Drive** begins at the visitors center and ends at a campground and trail head at an elevation of 10,000 feet. From there, you can hike several marked trails. The visitors center on SR 488 is open 8am-5pm daily all year and contains displays describing the Great Basin's plant and animal life, geologic development, and history.

The White Pine Chamber of Commerce is at 636 Aultman St., Ely, NV 89301 (phone 702-289-8877).

EUREKA

One of the oldest mining towns in the state, Eureka offers many original buildings that have survived and been restored, and the town has retained much of the flavor of its early days. If you close your eyes, you can almost hear a buckboard pulling away from Al's Hardware Store, in business since 1870, or cowboys having a fling on payday.

The most impressive structure is the **Eureka Courthouse**, gleaming with brass and flying a 44-star flag. It's also the starting point for a **walking tour** through town; a map is available at the assessor's office in the courthouse. A must-see is the *Eureka Sentinel* **Museum**, which houses the original printing apparatus of the newspaper, which began operating in 1870. Posters and reprints printed by the *Sentinel* in the 1870's and 80's are on display.

The Eureka Chamber of Commerce is in the newspaper building (phone 702-237-5484).

FALLON

Fallon, known nationwide for its Heart O'Gold cantaloupes (which are to melons what truffles are to mushrooms), looks much like an Iowa farm town. Wander through the tree-lined neighborhoods, wave at folks sitting in swings on the front porch, and you'll be tempted to whistle the theme from *Mayberry, R.F.D.*

The **Churchill County Museum** at 1050 S. Main St. (phone 702-423-3677) is considered one of the best in the state. It's full of exhibits showcasing the lives of the Indians of the region and turn-of-the-century rural life. There are significant collections of gems and minerals as well. It's open Mon-Sat 10am-5pm June-Sept; closed on Thursday the rest of the year. The museum offers free tours on the second and fourth Saturday of each month to **Grimes Point**, an archeological zone 12 miles east of town off U.S. 50. You can take a hike along petroglyph trails or explore Hidden Cave with a guide. Phone the museum for the schedule.

About 20 miles east is **Sand Mountain** and the Sand Springs Pony Express Station. Sand Mountain is one of the West's "singing mountains," made of shifting sands that make a low moaning sound when they move.

In July, Fallon celebrates with an **All-Indian Stampede and Pioneer Days**. On Labor Day at the **Heart O'Gold Cantaloupe Festival**, you can taste those luscious melons for yourself.

GABBS

The **Berlin-Ichthyosaur State Park**, 23 miles east of Gabbs on SR 844, contains fossils of extinct reptiles that once swam the ocean which covered Nevada over two million years ago. The park is open daily, and guided tours of the Ichthyosaur Fossil Shelter are given summer weekends at 10am, 2pm, and 4pm. Phone 702-964-2440 for hours during the remainder of the year. You'll find a visitors center and hiking trails at the park, and picnicking is permitted.

Also on the site is the ghost town of **Berlin**, with 13 preserved buildings. Signs explaining the site will guide you along a short tour through the buildings.

GENOA

Founded by one of Brigham Young's traders in 1849, Genoa is the oldest non-Indian permanent settlement in Nevada. Formerly known as Mormon Station, it's a quiet mix of pioneer grit and pastoral beauty. Be sure to visit the quaint downtown district, where the **oldest bar in Nevada** still serves thirsty travelers, and the **courthouse** built in 1865 is now a museum with a Virginia and Truckee Railroad display and replicas of an 1800's schoolroom, jail, kitchen, and courtroom. It's open from mid-May to mid-Oct 10am-4:30pm (phone 702-782-4325).

The **Mormon Station Historic State Monument**, located just off Hwy. 395, is a restored trading post and stockade built of logs in 1851, where emigrants stopped to rest before attempting to cross the Sierra Nevadas into California. There's also a small museum on the grounds. Open daily 10am-4:30pm from

May 1-Oct 15 (phone 702-782-2590).

Just south of Genoa, the **Lahontan National Fish Hatchery** on U.S. 395 raises cutthroat trout for stocking in western Nevada waters. Picnicking is permitted. Open daily 8am-3pm (phone 702-265-2425).

Should you be lucky enough to be in Genoa on a late September night with the harvest moon rising, don't miss the town's wonderful **Candy Dance**, a celebration that will make you think you've stepped back in time to a Saturday night in the 1860's. Women of the town dress in period costumes and pass out samples of their homemade candy, and bands play raucous music in every available corner. It's a wild celebration of the old days with cowboys and their ladies.

GOLDFIELD

Goldfield stands as a reminder of the boom-and-bust cycles of the state's mining industry. Founded in 1902 after the discovery of gold and silver, the town quickly grew to be the largest city in Nevada by 1906. As with most mining communities, when the ore ran out the people left, and over the years, floods and fires destroyed many parts of the town.

Many of the beautiful historic buildings remain, however. One of the best examples of Goldfield's rich past is the **Goldfield Hotel**, once the most luxurious between Kansas City and San Francisco. And the restored **Esmeralda County Courthouse** contains original Tiffany lamps.

During Goldfield's **Treasure Days** in August, the town honors its colorful past with unique events, including the world championship bar stool sitting contest. For more information, call the Goldfield Chamber of Commerce at 702-485-9957.

HAWTHORNE

Founded in 1880 as a point on the Carson and Colorado Railroad line, Hawthorne today is one of the country's largest ammunition depots. The **Mineral County Museum** details the region's history with Indian artifacts, old household articles, and archeological specimens. It's open Tue-Sat 11am-5pm from April-Oct; noon-4pm the rest of the year (phone 702-945-5142).

Just north of Hawthorne, **Walker Lake**, the traditional home of the Paiutes, is noted for its fine fishing. During the summer, you'll find fishing derbies and boat races on the lake.

A short drive from Hawthorne brings you to the ghost towns of **Bodie** and **Rawhide**. Bodie, off U.S. 395, has almost 200 buildings intact and looks as if its residents had vanished last night. Though nothing has been restored, the buildings have been treated to prevent further decay.

HENDERSON

Henderson is on SR 147, the scenic road that follows the Lake Mead shoreline.

Near Henderson and only 15 minutes from the Las Vegas Strip, the **Ethel M Chocolate Factory** creates some of America's finest gourmet chocolates — right in the middle of the desert! The factory is open daily 8:30am-7pm, and you may wander without a guide through the rooms. Don't go to the factory hungry; the smell is enough to turn you into a chocolate maniac. Free samples are offered, too. Outside the factory, there's a 2.5-acre **cactus garden** with over 350 types of cacti, succulents, and desert plants from the Southwest and other deserts of the world. This great attraction is on the Boulder Highway. Turn on Sunset Rd., then turn into Green Valley Business Park and go left on Cactus Garden Dr. The gardens keep the same hours as the chocolate factory. For more information, call 702-433-2500.

In April, Henderson celebrates **Industrial Days** with a parade, a carnival, a chili cook-off, and a beauty pageant. There's also a children's **Christmas parade** in December and the annual **Henderson Expo** in October.

LAS VEGAS

You might think money is free in Las Vegas. The town gleams 24 hours with glitzy flash and gambling palaces offering too-good-to-be-true deals and promotions designed to lure you past rows of inviting slot machines and card tables. Let's do the math: You get a free shrimp cocktail, two free drinks, and a free coffee mug. Total value about $10. The casino gets $50 of your quarters poured into their slots. Hmmmmm. That's an expensive coffee mug after all. But even non-gamblers can find plenty to do in Vegas, and many of the large casinos have attractions that cost nothing—as long as you can avoid temptation.

Circus Circus, the tent-shaped casino on the Strip (2880 Las Vegas Blvd. South, phone 702-734-0410 or 800-634-3450), features high-wire artists, clowns, and acrobats, all performing above the casino floor and accompanied by an ear-splitting brass band. At performance level, there's an observation gallery lined with food stands and carnival games. The circus area of the casino is open daily 11am-midnight. Children of all ages love it.

The Mirage is located at 3400 Las Vegas Blvd. S. (phone 702-791-7111 or 800-627-6667), in the center of tropically landscaped grounds. You can't miss it; just look for the volcano. That's right—an island three stories high is crowned with palm trees, cascading waterfalls, and a real volcano that erupts with a fiery blast every 15 minutes each evening. You can also watch dolphins cavort in a marine facility with a million gallons of seawater and manmade coral reefs. An aquarium 15 feet high and 40 feet long rises behind the hotel's front desk and holds small sharks and myriad iridescent fish. In the tiger habitat, three Siberian white tigers sprawl before a white tiled wall with a jungle motif and splash in a running stream. Trees and vines alive with orchids grow to the top of the two-story lobby, and sprinklers fill the air with a pleasant mist.

A gigantic castle with turrets and spires, **The Excalibur** is straight out of a children's coloring book. Cross the moat drawbridge and inside you'll see costumed employees joust and Lipizan stallions perform. The Magic Motion Machine is a theater with "active" seats that bounce up and down while a rafting trip down the Colorado River plays on the screen. The Excalibur is at 3850 Las Vegas Blvd. S. (phone 702-597-7700 or 800-939-7777).

At **Caesars Palace** (3570 Las Vegas Blvd. S., phone 702-731-7110 or 800-634-6661), "centurions"—muscle-bound young men in skimpy togas—leap onto a turning podium and pose motionless for a half-hour at a time, while Caesar and Cleopatra wander through the complex dispensing free medallions and gifts. Next door, the Forum Shops—a mall, Caesars-style—features a truly entertaining animated statue show of Bacchus, Apollo, Venus, and other figures from mythology, who mysteriously come to life every half-hour.

Las Vegas has recently seen quite a building boom, with a number of mega-casino hotels opening or soon to open. Each as its own unusual free attractions: The **Luxor**, a 30-story, black-glass pyramid, has an Egyptian-theme boat ride and unusual elevators. **Treasure Island**, next to the Mirage, offers a 15-minute battle six times a day between a British frigate and a pirate ship. (The pirates win.) The **Hard Rock Hotel/Casino** has an impressive array of artifacts and costumes from numerous musicians and rock stars. And at the **MGM Grand**—with a mere 5,005 rooms—you can feel like you're on a Hollywood movie set all day. And there's more to come...

Downtown in "Glitter Gulch," **Binion's Horseshoe** (128 Fremont St., phone 702-382-1600 or 800-622-6468) displays 100 U.S. $10,000 bills (that's a million bucks, cash) bound between plates of bulletproof glass. And the **Las Vegas Club Hotel and Casino** at 18 E. Fremont (phone 702-385-1664 or 800-634-6532) features the most complete collection of baseball memorabilia outside of Cooperstown.

At all the casinos, if you're over 21 you can watch **lounge entertainment**—some of it terrific, some of it hilariously bad—without paying a cent, simply by wandering through and standing in front of the various stage areas.

Beyond the gambling halls, Las Vegas offers a lot of free history and culture. The **Old Mormon Fort**, at Washington and

Feast your eyes on one million dollars cash at Binion's Horseshoe. (Allen Photographers)

Las Vegas Blvd., was built by the Mormons in 1855 for weary travelers bound for California. The fort later became a Union Pacific Railroad stop. Antiques re-create a 19th-century Mormon living room. Guided tours are available, but you can take a self-guided tour if you prefer. Open Thur-Mon from 9am-3:30pm in the summer and Monday and Saturday from 10am-4pm the rest of the year (phone 702-486-3511).

The University of Nevada's Las Vegas campus at 4505 Maryland Pkwy. offers free tours that include the **Donna Beam Fine Arts Gallery**, featuring modern art, and the **Barrick Museum of Natural History**, which details the natural history of southern Nevada and the Mojave Desert with exhibits of live desert animals and archeology. Both are open Mon-Fri from 9am-5pm and Sunday 1pm-5pm (phone 702-895-3893).

The **Las Vegas Museum of Natural History** (3700 Las Vegas Blvd. S., phone 702-384-3466) takes you on a journey through time, from the age of the dinosaurs to present-day wildlife. It's open daily from 9am-6pm.

The **Las Vegas Art Museum**, 3333 W. Washington (phone 702-647-4300) offers three galleries with changing exhibits by local and national artists. It's open 10am-3pm Mon-Sat and noon-3pm Sunday.

Drive west on Charleston Blvd., and you'll arrive at the **Red Rock Canyon** area, where you'll discover an information center and a 13-mile scenic loop that winds through unusual high-desert with lots of areas for hiking. Wild burros and bighorn sheep live in the canyon. Picnicking is allowed at Willow Spring, and you can camp at Oak Creek. The visitors center is open daily from 9am-4pm (phone 702-363-1921).

Mt. Charleston, to the north, is part of the Toiyabe National Forest and has an elevation of 12,000 feet. **Kyle** and **Lee Canyons** offer a cool escape from the heat of a Las Vegas summer and a wonderland of snow in the winter. There are several camping and picnic sites, and hiking trails lead to many areas of great natural beauty. Those with the endurance to climb to the top will be rewarded with bristlecone pines and incredible views.

Annual events in Las Vegas include an **All-Indian Powwow** in April (Native American dancing and festivities), **Helldorado Days** in May (re-creation of Old West styles and celebrations), and the **Fairshow** in late October (hot air balloon races, a chili cook-off, a bicycle relay, and softball tournaments).

The Las Vegas Chamber of Commerce's address is 3150 S. Paradise Rd., Las Vegas, NV 89109 (phone 702-892-0711).

The green valley of **Pahrump**, about an hour west of Las Vegas, is often a surprise to travelers and makes a lovely day trip. Area farmers get four crops a year from their alfalfa fields, and the valley is a pleasant change from the southern Nevada desert. Pahrump is the home of Nevada's only **winery**, which offers tastings and tours. In September, the town hosts a **Harvest Festival** with a parade and a barbecue.

LAUGHLIN

Nevada's newest gambling boomtown, Laughlin is on the Colorado River just above Davis Dam. As in Las Vegas, some of the casinos provide free attractions, and all offer free **ferry rides** across the river. Originally established to eliminate the drive from Bullhead City, AZ across Davis Dam to Laughlin, the ferries grew so popular that they continued even after a nearby bridge opened.

The **Ramada Express** offers a mile-long train ride with great views of the town, the river, the mountains and the desert. The fare is one smile. The classic car collection at the **Riverside Hotel and Casino** features over 80 rare and historic autos. It's open daily.

A self-guided tour of **Davis Dam** is available weekdays from 9am-4pm. Numerous displays explain how the dam's five turbines generate electricity. Water pours through the spillways at 214,000 cubic feet per second.

Grapevine Canyon, north off Hwy. 63, is 10 miles from the dam. Turn at Christmas Tree Pass and you'll find yourself on a clearly marked trail leading to a stream and steep cliffs filled with ancient Indian petroglyphs.

Laughlin's **River Days** began in 1982 as a tribute to the town's founder, Don Laughlin. Held in May each year, the event includes a parade, a soap box derby, a 10K run, street dances, and a carnival. The **RiverFlight Balloon Festival** in October features over 100 pilots and a spectacular "night glow." For more details, call the Laughlin Chamber of Commerce at 702-298-2214 (or 800-227-5245).

LOVELOCK

One of Nevada's architectural oddities is Lovelock's **Pershing County Courthouse**, the only round courthouse in use in the country. The city's huge park, shaded with 80-year-old trees, surrounds the courthouse.

West of town, the **Humboldt Sink**, a huge marsh, was home to native people 4,000 years ago who hunted around what was then an enormous, deep lake. Archeological discoveries at **Lovelock Cave** provided the first scientific data on the life of these Great Basin people. For directions to the cave and information about the town and region, stop at the **Pershing County Museum**, housed in a restored 19th-century building called the Marzen House. At the west end of Cornell Ave. (exit 105 off I-80), the house has displays of Paiute Indian artifacts and pioneer memorabilia. The Chamber of Commerce is also located here. It's open Mon-Sat 9am-4pm April-Nov; Mon-Fri 9am-1:30pm the rest of the year (phone 702-273-7213).

OVERTON

Mormon pioneers founded Overton just north of a settlement known as the Lost City. The **Lost City Museum of Archeology** contains Indian relics excavated from area pueblos that date back 10,000 years. On the museum grounds, several pit dwellings and pueblo-type structures have been built on the original foundations. The museum is open daily 8:30am-4:30pm (phone 702-397-2193).

The **Valley of Fire State Park**, 14 miles southwest of Overton on SR 169, derives its name from the brilliant red sandstone formations created by shifting sands 150 million years ago. The jagged walls often appear to be on fire when they reflect the sun's rays. Anasazi farmers and basket makers lived in the valley from 300 B.C. to 1150 A.D., and examples of their rock art can be found at several sites, especially **Atlatl Rock**, which is covered with prehistoric petroglyphs. Also visit **Mouse Tank**, a natural basin that collects rainwater, named after a reclusive Indian who used the area as a hide-out. The visitors center provides exhibits on the geology, ecology, and history of the park and is open daily from 8:30am-4:30pm (phone 702-397-2088). There are shaded picnic areas and many hiking trails.

PIOCHE

At its peak in the 1870's, Pioche was considered one of the toughest towns in the Old West. According to local legend, over 70 people were buried in the town's cemetery before anyone died of natural causes. The marker on one grave reads "Fanny Peterson, July 12, 1872. They loved to death did them part. He killed her." A walk though town will show you many historic buildings, and markers describe the history of each. Be sure to take a tour of the **Million Dollar Courthouse**, named because it cost the county about a million dollars after decades of corruption and mismanagement. Only 25 years after completion, the building and the land were sold for the grand sum of $150. The restored Courthouse now contains a small museum and is open for tours daily.

The **Lincoln County Historical Museum** on Main St. features interesting exhibits about the area's past with tools, furniture, and clothing. It's open daily 10am-4pm; closed holidays (phone 702-962-5207).

Spring Valley State Park, 18 miles east of Pioche, makes an excellent spot for fishing and hiking. And eight miles south of Pioche is the magnificent **Cathedral Gorge State Park**, a canyon lined with unusual clay formations carved by wind and erosion into a collection of fluted walls and towers that resemble church spires. There's an interpretive trail through the formations, a scenic overlook, and protected picnic areas.

RACHEL

This dusty little town is Mecca for believers in UFO's and extraterrestial visitors. Highway 375 has been named the **Extraterrestial Highway** and features "alien-friendly" road signs. In Rachel, be sure to stop at the **Little A'Le'Inn** and visit with the owner, who loves to talk about the strange sightings in the area. Some people believe the government is housing an alien craft and crew in "Area 51" nearby. If you want to take a drive through the Twilight Zone, call 800-638-2328 to get a free kit with the history of the area, a map, and an itinerary.

RENO

Known as the "Biggest Little City in the World," Reno is much more than a gambling town. You can find its more sedate side at the rose gardens in **Idlewild Park** along the Truckee River. On Monday, Wednesday, and Friday at noon in the summer, **Wingfield Park** downtown hosts band concerts. A tree-lined river walk connecting the two parks is a pleasant spot to rest with its benches, waterfalls, and murals depicting the early days of the city. There are evening band concerts on Island Ave. at the river walk from 7pm-10pm, and at the University on the Quad from 6pm-8pm during the summer.

Several of the casinos and local businesses sponsor free attractions. **Fitzgerald's Hotel Casino**, downtown on Virginia St. (phone 702-785-3300 or 800-648-5022), has a collection of lucky objects from around the world, including the only Blarney Stone ever to leave Ireland. **Circus Circus** (500 N. Virginia St., phone 702-329-0711 or 800-648-5010) has high-wire aerial acts, jugglers, and clowns that can be seen from a circular mezzanine above the casino floor. The **Silver Legacy Resort Casino** (407 N. Virginia St., phone 702-329-4777 or 800-687-8733) is housed inside the world's largest composite dome, with a mural that depicts Reno's dramatic skies. The casino features a variety of collections, including a stagecoach and antique planes, trains, and cars.

Antiques buffs and gamblers will be fascinated by the first three-reel slot machine, scores of other antique slots, and a collection of horse-drawn vehicles on display at the **Liberty Belle Saloon**, 4250 S. Virginia, adjacent to the Reno Convention Center (phone 702-825-1776). Open 4:30pm-11pm daily.

The **Lake Mansion**, home of Reno's founder Myron Lake, has been completely restored and is a treasure of early Nevada history. It's on South Virginia St. at the Reno Convention Center and open 8am-5pm Mon-Fri.

The **Nevada Historical Society Museum and Library** has a collection of baskets by Dat-So-La-Lee, a turn-of-the-century Washoe Indian considered the finest basket weaver in the country. Indian artifacts, mining antiques, and a lot more can be seen from 10am-5pm, Mon-Sat. The Museum is adjacent to the University of Nevada on North Virginia St. (phone 702-688-1190).

The **Church Fine Arts Building** on the University campus presents changing exhibits of contemporary art (open Mon-Fri 9am-4pm). Also on campus, the **Mineral Museum** at the Mackey School of Mines contains geological collections and exhibits on mining procedures. It's open Mon-Fri 8am-5pm; closed holidays (phone 702-784-6987).

Take a break from gambling and history and relax by **Virginia Lake**, where the ducks have the right-of-way. The lake is a bird refuge, but you'll find fitness stations, a jogging path, picnic areas, and a playground. To get there, go south on Virginia St., right on Plumb Lane, then west on Lakeside Dr.

Annual events in Reno include the **International Kite Festival** in April at Rancho San Rafael Park, with kite-flying demonstrations and a kite-building clinic. **Hot August Nights**, a celebration of America's love affair with the 1950's, features a classic car parade, lots of music, and street dances. It's held the first week in August. The **Great Reno Balloon Race**, with brilliant balloons ascending north of downtown, begins in early September in conjunction with the **Reno National Championship Air Races**, the only worldwide event featuring all four race classes: unlimited, Formula One, AT-6, and bi-planes. Military jet displays, aerobatics, and skywriters are also featured.

The Reno Chamber of Commerce is at 4590 S. Virginia, Reno, NV 89502 (phone 702-827-7366 or 800-367-7366).

SPARKS

Reno's twin city, **Sparks**, boasts a **Victorian Square** on B Street, the main street downtown. The **Sparks Heritage Museum**, open Wed-Sun from 1pm-5pm (phone 702-355-1144), is there, along with an outdoor railroad exhibit and special events year-round. In October, you can watch the **Great Race West**, with vintage cars in two classes — pre-1937 and 1937-59 — racing for prizes. Also in October, Sparks celebrates **Oktoberfest** with German music, dancing, arts and crafts, a keg-rolling contest, and a polka contest. A **Christmas Parade** and tree-lighting ceremony highlight December with caroling, crafts, and entertainment, all in Victorian style. And on May 5, Sparks hosts a **Cinco de Mayo** celebration at Victorian Square, featuring mariachis, dancing, and lots of great food. Call 702-353-2291 for more information.

Pyramid Lake, 33 miles northeast of Sparks, is a starkly beautiful high-desert lake — and one of the last remnants of a prehistoric sea that once covered Nevada and Utah. Surrounded by sandstone mountains, its waters are interrupted by weird rock islands jutting into the sky. The lake is on the Paiute Indian Reservation, the 475,000-acre home of the tribe. Pyramid Lake's north end is sacred to the Paiutes and off-limits to visitors. The area, full of campgrounds, hiking trails, and beaches, is also home to a **fish hatchery** where the prehistoric cui-ui fish are raised. Open daily 9am-11am and 1pm-3pm, the hatchery also breeds cutthroat trout (phone 702-476-0160).

TAHOE

Lake Tahoe is the largest alpine lake in North America and the second deepest. The lake's **Emerald Bay** must be one of the most photographed spots on earth. Nestled in the southwest corner of the lake, the bay is surrounded by the peaks of the Sierras, out of which **Eagle Falls** gushes. A hiking trail takes you up to the falls and a small fishing lake or down the steep slopes to **Vikingsholm**. This massive stone castle, built by a millionaire in the 1920's, is complete with towers, turrets, and antiques. The 38-room mansion has been called the finest example of Scandinavian architecture in North America. It's open June-Labor Day from 10am-4pm (phone 916-541-3030).

The **Tallac Historic Site** on SR 89 consists of three 19th-century estates. The Tevis-Pope estate is the oldest, built in 1894. The middle house, a replica of a Belgian hunting lodge, serves as an Indian museum, with the outbuildings used as a gallery and workshop for traveling artists. The Heller estate is called "Valhalla" after the great hall of the Viking afterlife. Picnicking is permitted on the grounds, and guided tours are available. From Memorial Day to Labor Day, it's open Mon-Sat 11am-3pm. The visitors center is open Mon-Fri 9am-6pm (phone 916-542-4166).

TONOPAH

In 1900, a prospector named Jim Butler was caught in a sudden rain storm and sought shelter under a ledge near what is now Tonopah. While waiting for the sky to clear, he removed some ore samples from the rock. The samples turned out to be almost pure silver, and Butler's find sparked a mining boom in the state.

With dozens of historic structures and mine ruins, Tonopah is a paradise for history buffs. Begin your tour with a visit to the town's **Central Museum** (Logan Field Rd., phone 702-482-9676), one of the Southwest's best small museums, with excellent exhibits about the area's mines, railroads, and boom towns. From May to September, the museum is open daily 9am-5pm and Tue-Sat from 11am-5pm the rest of the year.

Each Memorial Day weekend, Tonopah celebrates **Jim Butler Days** in honor of the town's founder. Events include camel and burro races, barbecues, parades, and the state championship rock-drilling contest. And if your name is Jim Butler, you can be a grand marshal in the parade. Just contact the Tonopah Chamber of Commerce (702-482-3859).

VIRGINIA CITY

A popular day trip from the Reno-Tahoe area, Virginia City has been called "the liveliest ghost town in the West." Born of the Comstock silver bonanza of 1859, Virginia City's riches built San Francisco and financed the Union during the Civil War.

The great fire of 1875 almost destroyed the city, but most of it was rebuilt and the town looks much as it did in its heyday. From the well-worn board sidewalks of the main street to the grand mahogany bars and crystal chandeliers in the saloons, it's easy to close your eyes and imagine the Wild West in all its glory and decadence. Over 750 miles of tunnels wind beneath Virginia City; the honeycombs of square-set timbers that made the mining of the lode possible also underpin the city and keep it stable on its mountainous site.

Stroll the streets, listen to the honky-tonk music, and take in the history. The Virginia City Visitors Bureau on C Street shows a slide presentation on the history of the town. Call 702-847-0177 for the schedule. And the Chamber of Commerce (phone 702-847-0311) across the street in the V&T Railroad car has brochures with all kinds of information on the area.

Notable residents have included Bret Harte and Samuel Clemens, a.k.a. Mark Twain. Both worked as reporters for the *Territorial Enterprise*, Nevada's first newspaper, still publishing today. At the newspaper building, the **Mark Twain Museum of Memories** has nickelodeons, telephones, and late-1800's fashions. An impersonator brings Twain to life. It's open daily 10am-5pm from May-Oct; 10am-4pm the rest of the year (phone 702-847-0454).

The **Nevada State Fire Museum** at 51 C Street (the main street) displays antique fire wagons dating to 1839. Uniforms, photos, and firefighting accessories are also in the collection, all relics from the volunteer days of the department. It's open daily in the summer from 10am-5pm (phone 702-847-0717).

St. Mary's in the Mountains, a church built on the site of a church destroyed in the 1875 fire, has been restored and is open daily in the summer and on weekends the rest of the year.

Journalists called the **Fourth Ward School** the pride and glory of the Comstock when it was built in 1876. One of the nation's last schools of this size and type still standing, it offers a comprehensive look at life during the early days. Two classrooms have been restored to their original state. It's open daily from 9am-4pm in the summer.

A tour of Virginia City should end with a trip to the **cemetery** at the edge of town. The stories behind the crumbling headstones tell of the hardships and danger that characterized the lives of the early residents: women who died in childbirth, men killed in barroom brawls over a bit of silver, and children who died of illnesses we consider trivial today. It's a grim history lesson and a peaceful place at last for those who created the legacy of Virginia City.

The town is always lively, but especially so in September, when it hosts the **International Camel Races**, a re-creation of a pursuit popular during the Comstock's bonanza days. The most popular event of the year, the races originated after a fictitious report of camel races appeared in the local paper. The race to the finish line and the antics of the stubborn beasts make for a hilarious spectator sport. There are ostrich races daily at noon as well. Call the Chamber for the dates of each year's event.

WELLS

Originally called Humboldt Wells, this area was an important stop for pioneers following the California Emigrant Trail. Ruts left by the iron-wheeled wagons still scar the land nearby.

The town was established in 1869 by the Central Pacific Railroad, and travelers will find a historic commercial district adjacent to the tracks. South of Wells, Highway 93 runs almost parallel to the Ruby Mountains and intersects with SR 489, which leads to the historic mining town of **Cherry Creek**, where you'll find old miners' shacks, stone and brick walls and foundations, large cemeteries, a small museum (open only on weekends), and other ghosts from the past.

WINNEMUCCA

Winnemucca's recorded history began in the 1840's in the Humboldt River Valley, which became an avenue for the pioneers traveling west. But long before the whites came, the river was important to the Indians as a source of food and willows for basket-making. Indeed, Winnemucca was named after an Indian chief and means "one moccasin." A trading post opened in 1853, followed by a ferry and then a toll bridge. In at least one canyon, you can see the ruts carved by thousands of covered wagons over a century ago. Local legend tells of emigrant children in 1845 tossing pebbles into blue buckets that were hanging from their wagon. The pebbles were gold nuggets, and although hundreds have searched, the fabled Blue Bucket Gold Mine has never been found.

A great free attraction in town is the **First National Bank**, the last bank robbed by Butch Cassidy and the Sundance Kid. Completely restored, you can see memorabilia of the event from 9am-4pm daily.

On the first weekend in June, Winnemucca hosts a **Draft Horse and Mule Show**, with performance driving, working classes, and racing. Also in June, the **Basque Festival** celebrates the influence of the Basques in northern Nevada with a parade, sporting events, traditional Basque dancing, and the colorful *Meza Santuko Otoitzak*, a Basque mass.

Perhaps the most famous of Winnemucca's annual events is the **Western Art Roundup**, held on Labor Day weekend at the Heritage Museum in the Winnemucca Convention Center. A wine-tasting and "quick draw" contest highlight the three-day event, with Western artists and poets on hand to share their stories of life on the open range. The most coveted prize is a pair of silver spurs, given for the work judged best in the "Buckaroo Heritage" category. There's even an award for the most high-spirited drawing!

The **Humboldt County Museum** in the same building tells of the region's history with hundreds of antiques. On display are many items donated by area ranchers and nationally known artists. The museum is open on weekends from 8am-

4pm (phone 702-623-2912).

The Winnemucca Chamber of Commerce is at 30 W. Winnemucca Blvd. (phone 702-623-2225). They have a brochure describing a self-guided tour of the town.

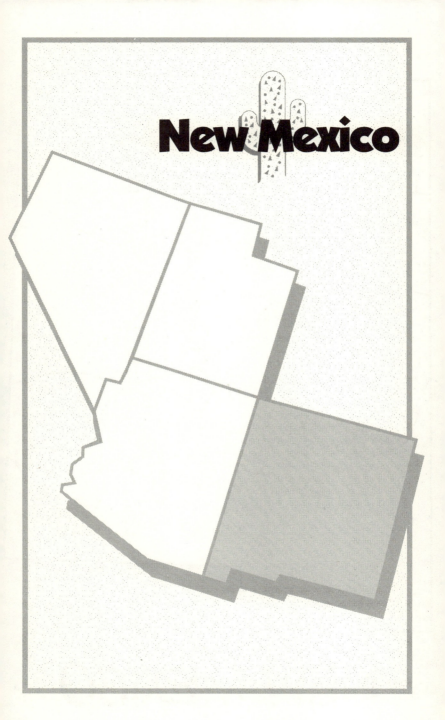

New Mexico

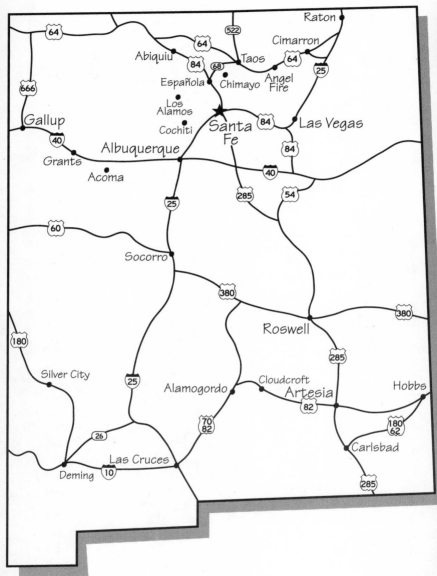

NEW MEXICO

New Mexico

The area now known as New Mexico has long been a source of myths, tall tales, mystics, and average people who become legends. There are even legends about how the legends began. The very appearance of the state stimulates the imagination: vast stretches of land guarded by enormous, silent rock formations, ghost towns and Indian spirit places, the old Santa Fe Trail and the paths of the conquistadors. In "The Land of Enchantment," dirt-brown cliffs adopt myriad colors as they tower against an azure sky, and ordinary men have become heroes.

New Mexico's earliest inhabitants settled in the area some 12,000 years ago. Spanish explorers arrived in the 1500's seeking treasure but finding only mica in the adobe. Missionaries, determined to convert the Indians to Christianity, followed the conquistadors. When Mexico declared independence from Spain in 1821, New Mexico became a province of the new nation, but trade with the U.S. along the Santa Fe Trail made settlers look to Washington, D.C. for government. War erupted between Mexico and the U.S. in 1846, and Americans occupied Santa Fe and declared the area part of the Union. It became the Territory of New Mexico in 1850, along with present-day Arizona. The railroad arrived in the late 1870's and launched economic growth, resulting in statehood in 1912.

World War II brought a second boom: the government's scientific research, which continues today in the mountains and canyons surrounding Los Alamos.

Author D. H. Lawrence called New Mexico "the greatest experience from the outside world I have ever known." Many visitors agree, especially nature enthusiasts who can't help but speak in superlatives when describing the state's splendor. Natural treasures await at every turn, from sandstone cliffs in the north to vast seas of grass in the south. Six national forests lie entirely within the state, protecting thousands of square miles. Hiking trails crisscross the mountains, and hunting and world-class fishing are found on most public lands. Renowned for boating, rafting, and kayaking, New Mexico is also perfect for hang gliding. Near Hobbs, soaring enthusiasts have discovered air currents so strong they run all the way to Kansas! Rock collectors can help themselves at Rockhound State Park near Deming, and throughout the state, archeologists welcome volunteers to help them uncover the past. In the national monuments, you can walk worn Indian paths and climb a *kiva* ladder into prehistoric cave dwellings.

Snow once drove hunters and mountain men into the low country. Today, winter turns the heights into a skier's wonderland. Scattered in the Sangre de Cristo mountains are the internationally-known ski areas of Taos, Santa Fe, and Angel Fire. Cross-country skiers will find groomed trails and miles of national forest.

With the changing seasons, there's always reason for a celebration somewhere. Festivities abound in New Mexico, commemorating the reconquest of the state by Diego de Vargas, the shooting of Billy the Kid, the planting of corn, the harvesting of apples, and much more. Some of the events are on a grand scale — the Albuquerque International Balloon Fiesta draws hundreds of thousands. Others are smaller but equally fascinating, like the Great American Duck Race in Deming.

There's been a strong Indian presence in New Mexico for thousands of years. Petroglyphs and pictographs still grace cliff walls and boulders throughout the state, and dramatic ruins at

Bandolier Monument and Chaco Canyon mark once-thriving cities. The state's 19 Indian pueblos have traditional dances scheduled nearly every month; the most spectacular is in Gallup in early August. Or, you can witness ceremonies surrounding the puberty rituals of the Mescalero Apaches near Ruidoso in July. Visitors to Indian country are welcome to observe the dances and enjoy the traditional arts and crafts, but please be courteous. The villages are primarily homes and spiritual centers, not tourist attractions. Each tribe has its own regulations regarding photos, tape recordings, fishing, and camping, so always ask first. If you attend dances, remember that each dance is a prayer, and refrain from talking during dances or applauding afterwards.

Religious celebrations occur often in traditional Catholic communities, along with special fiestas in honor of local patron saints. La Fiesta de Santa Fe in September commemorates the reconquest of the city in 1692. The burning of *Zozobra*, a 40-foot-high model of Old Man Gloom, is a spectacular highlight of the festival, said to banish all cares and woes. New Mexico's Spanish history is honored in several villages in late spring on *Cinco de Mayo*, a Mexican celebration of the defeat of the French Army near Puebla, Mexico in 1862. Cowboys and desperados also played a part in the state's heritage. Those curious about Billy the Kid can watch his exploits re-created in Lincoln in August, and Las Vegas (not the one with the showgirls and the slot machines) honors its iron horse past with Rails 'n Trails Days at the end of May. Deming, near the Mexican border, offers a fiddle contest in May and Butterfield Stage Days in July.

You'll find green chilies, the official state vegetable, in everything from salsa to jelly. The center of the chili industry is Hatch, just north of Las Cruces. In September, the smell of roasting chilies fills Hatch's countryside, as the town stages a festival featuring a fiddle contest, a cook-off, a *ristra*-making competition, and the crowning of a Green Chili Queen.

As the railroad — and later the automobile — opened the territory, New Mexico's art began to flourish. Word spread of incredibly clean light, friendly people, and colorful scenery, and soon colonies of writers, painters, and other creative types found Taos and Santa Fe. Indian artisans gained fame, and the forms came together in many galleries and shows. The most famous is the Santa Fe Indian Market. South of Santa Fe, the mining town of Madrid survived to become a creative haven whose annual events include a celebrated jazz festival.

The prospectors, conquistadors, desperados, and other legendary figures no longer hitch their horses by the saloons on Main Street, but their presence permeates New Mexico. A century ago, the Indians called it "the dancing ground of the sun." Piñon trees blanketing arid mesas, majestic mountains gripping the skies, a palette of hues at sunset, rushing streams, snow-covered slopes, adobe pueblos, bright fiestas, and warm hospitality — all create a state filled with wonders to behold.

ABIQUIU

Abiquiu was the birthplace of Father Antonio José Martinez, the priest who established the Southwest's first coeducational school. His lifelong crusade to educate people took him to Taos and into politics.

The **Ghost Ranch Living Museum**, 14 miles northwest of town on US 84, is operated by the Forest Service and stresses conservation education. Displays include native animals and plants, a miniature forest, and a geology exhibit. The museum is a branch of the New Mexico Museum of Natural History, so it often hosts traveling exhibits, too. And the Conference Center has a display of the official dinosaur of New Mexico, coelophysis, which was discovered on the ranch. Open Tue-Sun 8am-4pm (phone 505-685-4312).

ACOMA

A hugh monolith, called by many **Enchanted Mesa**, stands 400 feet above the plain a few miles east of Acoma. According to local legend, it was once an ancestral village. One day, when the people were tending to the fields in the valley, a violent storm washed away all access to the mesa, leaving a young girl

The Mission of San Estevan del Rey in Acoma.

and her grandmother stranded on top. Rather than die of starvation, the two leapt from the cliff walls.

The location of Acoma (a.k.a. Sky City) was considered ideal for defense. Archeologists say Acoma was occupied until 1150 A.D. A visitors center at the base of the mesa offers a free museum exhibit. Non-Indians are not allowed on the mesa top without a guide.

ALAMOGORDO

In July 1945, in a remote section of the White Sands Missile Range near Alamogordo, the first manmade atomic explosion sent a huge mushroom cloud billowing 40,000 feet high. The crater at **Trinity Site** bears mute testimony to the beginning of the atomic age. There are tours on the first Saturday in April and the first Saturday in October. You must first write the

Public Affairs Office, Bldg. 122, White Sands Missile Range, NM 88002, or call (phone 505-678-1134).

The **Space Center**, just off US 54, is a large complex containing the International Space Hall of Fame, a space theater, the Stapp Air and Space Park, and the Astronaut Memorial Garden. Exhibits honor space pioneers from many nations, and an outdoor display includes launch vehicles and spacecraft. It's open daily from 9am-5pm. The grounds and gardens are free, but there's a small charge for the Space Hall and the theater (phone 505-437-2840 or 800-545-4021).

Three Rivers Petroglyph Site is one of the nation's largest groups of prehistoric writing, with more than 5,000 examples thought to have been inscribed from 900-1400 A.D. A trail leads through the site, and camping and picnicking are permitted. It's open 24 hours (phone 505-525-8228).

The Chamber of Commerce is located at 1301 White Sands Blvd., Alamogordo, NM 88310 (phone 505-437-6150).

ALBUQUERQUE

Between 1850 and 1875, numerous forts were established in the Southwest to protect the westward immigrants. Albuquerque, a supply center for those forts, had an established culture nearly 200 years old and so never experienced the lawless days of the frontier. Indeed, much of Albuquerque's appeal comes from its blend of many cultures.

There's a treasure trove of history hidden in the center of modern Albuquerque. The town was settled 70 years before the American Revolution, when King Philip of Spain gave colonists permission to take an area of the Rio Grande Valley, known today as **Old Town**. Now a historic zone, the area still looks much as it did centuries ago. Activities center around the picturesque plaza and focus on art, history, and tradition. A block from the plaza, the **Albuquerque Museum** (2000 Mountain St. NW, phone 505-243-7255), one of the country's first solar-heated museums, exhibits 400 years of local history—from the conquistadors to the present. The museum, which also offers an hour-long tour of Old Town, is open daily except

Monday, from 9am-5pm. The tours begin Tue-Sun at 11am.

The lives of many early settlers centered around religion, and the first building they erected was a small adobe chapel, **San Felipe de Neri Church**, still standing on the northwest corner of the plaza. The building, a mix of Victorian and adobe architecture, has been enlarged and remodeled several times, but the thick, original walls remain intact. The church is the hub of Old Town, and many descendants of the original inhabitants live in the surrounding buildings.

The Indian Pueblo Cultural Center presents free traditional Indian dances and art demonstrations every Saturday and Sunday. The dances begin at 11am and 2pm, the art demonstrations at 10am and 4pm. The center is at 2401 12th St. (phone 505-843-7270).

Atomic energy and its sources are at the heart of the **National Atomic Museum**, the only one of its kind in the country. The museum features an exhibition on the Manhattan Project, the government program centered in New Mexico that developed and tested the first atomic bomb. Don't miss the documentary film **Ten Seconds That Shook the World**, shown four times a day (phone 505-845-6670 for times). An hour-long tour explores the development of nuclear weapons, and colorful exhibits detail solar power and other applications of energy research. The museum is open daily 9am-5pm; visitors must obtain a pass from the military guards at the Visitors Center (Kirtland Air Force Base at Wyoming Blvd.).

Three area vineyards offer free tours and tastings. **Anderson Valley Vineyards**, 4920 Rio Grande Blvd. (phone 505-344-7266), offers samples of 12 wines and tours of the vineyards daily from noon-5:30pm. At **Sandia Shadows Vineyard and Winery**, tour guides explain the wine-making process. It's seven miles north of town on Tramway Blvd. off San Rafael (phone 505-856-1006) and open Wed-Sun 1pm-5pm and Sat 10am-5pm. The **Las Nutrias Vineyard and Winery**, an award-winning winery in the scenic village of Corrales, is minutes from downtown Albuquerque. For details, call 505-897-7683.

Another interesting tour is available at the **New Mexico**

Candle Company, which offers handmade candles, each signed by the maker, that emphasize Southwestern designs. Open Mon-Fri, 9am-5pm (12 20th St. SE in Rio Rancho, phone 505-891-2366).

The **University of New Mexico**, situated on a 640-acre campus two miles east of downtown on Central Ave. (US 66), is home to several museums. Hundreds of colorful minerals, meteorites, moon rocks, and fossils are on display at the **Museum of Geology and Meteoritics** (open 8am-4:30pm Mon-Fri). The **UNM Art Museum** features exhibits of painting and photography from the 19th century through the present (open Tue-Fri 9am-4pm). The **Jonson Gallery** houses the work of Raymond Jonson, a major modernist painter who created the gallery as a residence and archive for contemporary art. His art is displayed June-August; other artists' work can be seen the rest of the year (open Tue-Fri 9am-4pm). The **Maxwell Museum of Anthropology** emphasizes native culture of the Southwest (open Mon-Fri 9am-4pm).

If you turn right at the corner of 6th and Central, you'll be on the fabled **Route 66**. At 5th and Central, stop by the **KiMo Theater**, originally built for vaudeville acts. An art deco interpretation of American Indian motifs, the KiMo offers a lobby with murals and fanciful plaster ceilings from the 1920's. It's open 8am-5pm Mon-Fri, and admission is free (unless there's a performance).

In the same neighborhood, at 5th and Marquette, there's a heroic **bronze statue** by Native American artist Alan Houser, and the **Art Garage**, which houses public art works (open 7am-7pm Mon-Fri). Go east on Central, and you'll come to the Huning Highlands district, home to the **Special Collections Library** at Edith and Central, which houses the Don Quixote Portfolio, illustrated by several of the city's most successful artists (open 9am-5:30pm Wed, Fri, and Sat).

Just across Central from the University is the **Tamarind Lithography Institute and Gallery** at 108 Cornell Ave. SE. The gallery is open 9am-5pm Mon-Fri, and free tours are offered on the first Friday of each month at 1pm. Reservations are recommended (phone 505-277-3901).

One of the best times to visit Albuquerque is during the **International Balloon Fiesta**, the largest ballooning event in the world. A "balloon glow," which involves hundreds of balloons inflated at dusk, occurs the first Sunday evening of the fiesta. Visitors can see the Special Shapes Rodeo, featuring dozens of bizarre and promotional balloons, as well as parachute teams and stunt flying. A true must-see event, the festival runs the first two weeks in October. Call the Albuquerque Chamber of Commerce (800-284-2282) for details.

Another gorgeous spectacle, the **Christmas Eve Lumineria Tour** winds along a route lit by thousands of candles placed in small brown bags filled with sand. The bags line streets, buildings, and windows, creating a soft wonderland of light.

In May, Albuquerque hosts the **Festival of the Arts**, with over 150 events throughout the city, including gospel concerts and a literary fair. Call 505-842-9918 for details.

The Turquoise Trail, a drive famous for its beauty, travels the back roads of Sandia Crest through the Cibola National Forest to the summit (10,678 feet). The crest reveals a rustic landscape and an awesome view of Albuquerque. Back again on North 14, you'll pass through Golden, once a turquoise-mining town. Madrid is next, a ghost town turned artist's haven, with weathered old houses and the original town jail. Cerillos, just north, is another ghost town that has been revitalized with a frontier trading post and displays of mining equipment. The village, with its tree-lined street dotted with small shops, has often been used in Western films.

Three sites with ruins of Indian pueblos and missions are part of the **Salinas Pueblo Missions National Monument**, reached by driving east on I-40 to the Tijeras exit, then turning south on NM 14 through the Manzano Foothills. You'll pass through four old Hispanic villages: Chilili, Tajique, Torreón, and Manzano. A paved road at Punta de Agua leads into the ruins, which stand as mute tribute to the Indians and missionaries who braved the elements to establish a community. The ruins are simply astonishing. **Ab**, a former Tompiro Indian village, has the circa-1620 **Church of San Gregorio de Abo** — one of the few surviving examples of medieval architecture in

Balloons fill the sky during Albuquerque's International Balloon Fiesta. (photo: Terry Moore)

the U.S. Most of the churches were destroyed after an Indian rebellion in 1680. Seven remain today; two were rebuilt, and the others are national monuments. **Gran Quivira** contains 21 mound houses dating to 1300; you can visit 300 rooms and six *kivas*. You'll also see the churches of San Isidro, begun in 1629, and San Buenaventura, begun in 1659. **Quaral** preserves ten pueblo house mounds and the remains of a circa-1630 church and convent. A museum there displays a model of the old church and a collection of pottery. All three sites are open daily 9am-5pm. A visitors center on US 60 in Mountainair offers slide shows and an art exhibit (phone 505-847-2585).

To visit a living Indian pueblo, take I-25 south to the signs for **Isleta Pueblo**. Isleta has one of the oldest mission churches in the Southwest: the **Church of San Augustin**, built in 1613. The pueblo, which covers over 200,000 acres, has 3,800 members and is the largest of the Tiwa-speaking pueblos. A delicious part of a visit is the bread the women bake in outdoor beehive ovens (*hornos*). Isleta artisans also make fine jewelry, pottery, and clothing. Two feast days honor St. Augustine; Aug. 24 is the big feast, while Sept. 4 is called the "little feast" by tribal members. You may take pictures during non-feast days in the area of the church, but only of the buildings, not the people. Open daily 9am-6pm (phone 505-869-3111).

You'll find evidence of a much earlier civilization at the **Petroglyph National Monument** (4735 Unser Blvd. N.W., phone 505-839-4429). A 17-mile-long lava slope contains over 15,000 drawings scratched into the rock, the earliest of which date to 1300 A.D.

Northwest of Albuquerque are the pueblos of Zia and Santa Ana and the Spanish village of San Ysidro. **Zia**, established in the 17th century, is perhaps best known for its ancient sun symbol showing four rays emanating in four directions. A symbol of friendship, it's the official state emblem of New Mexico. Potters from this village have a reputation for excellence, using traditional geometric designs and animal motifs on white backgrounds. The annual **Our Lady of Assumption Feast Day** is celebrated on Aug. 15 with a corn dance. The pueblo is open during daylight hours but may be closed during some religious events (phone 505-867-3304).

The old village of **Santa Ana** is open to the public only on Jan. 1 and 6, Easter Sunday, June 24 and 29, July 25 and 26, and Dec. 25-28. The new village, **Ta-Ma-Ya**, is open 10am-4pm Tuesday and Thursday, and noon-4pm on Sunday. Two miles north of NM 44 off NM 313, the pueblo specializes in organic and blue corn products. No photos are allowed.

Jeméz hosts two well-known feasts. On Aug. 2, the feast of Our Lady of the Angels is marked by the Old Pecos Bull Dance, and on Nov. 12, the tribe honors San Diego. Jeméz is open to visitors only on feast days, but you're welcome year-round at **Red Rock Scenic Area**, three miles north on NM 4. Fishermen love nearby Dragonfly Lake and Holy Ghost Springs; licenses are available on the site. While you can't take pictures in Jeméz, photographs are encouraged at Red Rock (phone 505-834-7359).

Brochures detailing self-guided tours through Albuquerque and the countryside are available at the Albuquerque Visitors Bureau, 121 Tijeras Ave. NE, Albuquerque, NM 87125 (phone 505-842-9918).

ANGEL FIRE

A resort community in the Moreno Valley of the Sangre de Cristo Mountains, Angel Fire features the **DAV Vietnam Veterans Memorial**, a revered landmark overlooking one of northern New Mexico's most beautiful valleys. The soaring, gull-like structure rises over 50 feet, and its mountain-top vantage yields magnificent views. On Memorial Day weekend, there's a candlelight vigil, chapel services, and guest speakers. The chapel is open 24 hours; the visitors center is open Tue-Sat 9am-6pm (phone 505-377-6900).

The **Cleveland Mill Historical Museum**, south of Angel Fire, was one of northern New Mexico's largest flour mills in the late 1800's. Restored to operating condition, the mill has artifacts, massive machinery, and exhibits that provide an opportunity to experience a little-known aspect of New Mexico's history.

It's open Memorial Day-Oct. 31 from 10am-5pm.

ARTESIA

Named after the area's artesian wells, Artesia offers the colorful **Heritage Walkway**, a line of murals through downtown that
gives a tour of the town's history. The **Artesia Historical Museum and Art Center** (505 W. Richardson Ave., phone 505-748-
2390) was built as a residence in 1904 and is now on the
National Register of Historic Places. The cobblestones used in
its construction were hauled from a small stream south of
town. The museum is devoted to local history, and the art center offers a collection of works by local artists. It's open Tue-Sat
8am-noon and 1pm-5pm (closed holidays).

CARLSBAD

Carlsbad was named after a local spring that is said to have
medicinal value. The **Pecos Flume** carries Pecos River water
from a lake through an irrigation canal and the river itself. Built
of wood in 1890, it was rebuilt in 1902 of concrete and was
once the largest concrete structure in the world.

The **Carlsbad Courthouse**, constructed in 1891, is one of the
most picturesque halls of justice in the Southwest. Cattle
brands of many old ranch families are carved in the dark wood
at each entrance. On the south lawn, an anti-aircraft gun used
in the South Pacific during World War II commemorates the
Eddy County men who fought at Bataan.

The **Family History Center**, an extension of the Salt Lake
Library in Utah, is a well-known genealogical research facility
with over 200 million names on file. It's open Tue-Fri 10am-
4pm (1200 Church St., phone 505-885-1368).

The **Carlsbad Museum and Art Center** displays minerals,
Southwestern art, Indian pottery, and pioneer artifacts. Open
Mon-Sat 10am-6pm (418 W. Fox, phone 505-887-0276).

The area around Carlsbad is spectacular, especially the
Guadalupe National Forest, which preserves the rugged
splendor of the Old West. You can see the mountains from 50
miles in any direction, and the canyons have an impressive

variety of plants and animals. In **McKittrick Canyon**, you can hike along a spring-fed stream; in the fall, the foliage turns its walls to gold. A self-guided nature trail begins at the entrance to the canyon. At **The Pinery**, you'll see the ruins of an old stagecoach station, built in 1858. The **Frijole Ranch** has the most substantial buildings of early ranching in the area. Maps and trail guides are available at the visitors center.

New Cave is 25 miles southwest of town on US 62; the last mile is unpaved, and a one-mile trail leads to the cave itself. This new part of Carlsbad Caverns has a variety of dramatic formations. Children under six are not permitted; bring a flashlight and water. A two-hour guided tour is offered every day at 9am and 2:30pm from May-Sept (reservations required; phone 505-785-2232).

CHIMAYO

The Spanish village of Chimayo—home of the Ortega family, famous for eight generations of weavers—is especially nice to visit in the fall, when the cottonwoods turn gold and *ristras* of red chilies dry in the sun.

In town, you'll find a *galleria* that's fun to browse, and a small restaurant with *al fresco* dining. The plaza, constructed in 1696, is one of the oldest surviving in the Southwest. **El Sanctuario de Nuestro Señor de Equipulas** is found at the east end of the village. According to pueblo legend, a farmer was instructed by a vision to dig for earth that had healing powers. He uncovered a cross and placed it inside an adobe chapel that he built in 1814. Today, pilgrims come to scoop handfuls of the earth from a pit inside the chapel. During Holy Week, over 10,000 people visit, and all but the weakest walk (many all the way from Albuquerque, almost 100 miles away). The chapel is open daily from 9am-4pm (phone 505-351-4889).

Chimayo is on SR 76—the "high road to Taos"—and two other well-known crafts villages are on the same road: **Cordova**, known for its wood-carvings, and **Truchas**, home to a family of master weavers. Visitors are welcome to watch the artists in their workshops from dawn to dusk on weekdays.

CIMARRON

The word *cimarrón* means "wild"—an apt description of the town in the 1880's. The local paper once reported, "Things are quiet. Nobody has been killed in three days." Billy the Kid and Black Jack Ketchum were among the town's early residents. The **St. James Hotel**, where Annie Oakley joined Buffalo Bill's Wild West Show, stands today, along with the old jail. Every July since 1922, cowboys have participated in a **rodeo**, and mountaineers take part in **Cimarron Days** each Labor Day.

The **Philmont Scout Ranch**, a 140,000-acre national camping center operated by the Boy Scouts of America, hosts thousands of teenagers each summer. Its headquarters has a museum with artifacts on regional history and art. The Seton Memorial Library, inside the museum, contains the art and library of Ernest Seton, the first Chief Scout of America. Philmont is open daily 8am-5pm from June-Aug (phone 505-376-2281).

CLOUDCROFT

The peaceful mountain village of Cloudcroft was founded in 1898 when a group of surveyors reached the summit of the Sacramento Mountains. The sight of one white cloud nestled among the pines inspired them to name the spot.

Surrounded by over a million acres of national forest at an elevation of 9,000 feet, Cloudcroft has four distinct seasons, so visitors can enjoy diverse activities. In the winter, you can skate at a unique outdoor rink, open seven days a week from 10am-8pm, and it's free if you bring your own skates. (Skates rent for $2.00, with no time limit.) The annual **Full Moon Skating Party** occurs in February with free hot chocolate, cider, and cookies. In the summer, try a hike on the **Osha Trail**, a mile west of town. It's an easy 2.5-mile walk, winding around the mountain through oak and fir trees — a great trek for a family. The ranger station has a map (open Mon-Sat 7:30am-4:30pm). Hardier hikers should explore the four-mile **Willie White Trail**, two miles south of town. The trail head and camping areas are free, and the trail is open in the winter for cross-country skiing. The summer offers wildflowers in the deep-green grass of the meadows, and autumn displays red oaks and golden aspen.

In town, visit the **Sacramento Mountains Historical Museum**, which recalls the town's early days with a pioneer village from the late 1800's, old farming and ranching tools, household items, clothing, and a wooden washing machine. It's open Tue-Sat 10am-4pm; closed Thanksgiving and Christmas.

About 17 miles south of town at the **Sacramento Peak Observatory**, the National Science Foundation conducts solar research. Free tours are available Saturdays from May-October.

Cloudcroft has many free annual events: a **Winter Carnival** in February, **Railroad and Logging Days** in May (with miniature trains, logging contests, and mountaineer displays), an outstanding **arts and crafts show** held on Memorial Day weekend, and June's **Western Roundup**, with a parade, a knife and gun show, a street dance, and a fiddling contest. At the end of June, the **Bluegrass Festival** offers a special afternoon performance in the park. A free **musical revue** is presented each summer in July, and **July 4th** festivities include a crafts fair, horseshoe tournament, and street dance. August hosts a three-day **songfest**, and Labor Day has a **Mariachi Festival**, with a *piñata* party for the kids. October brings **Oktoberfest** and **Aspencade**, a tour of aspen trees that ends with coffee around a campfire and a presentation by the Forest Service. At **Christmas**, there's a pet parade, a tree-lighting ceremony, an ice-sculpture contest, and a skating party.

COCHITI

Craftsmen at this Keresan pueblo are famous for their drums, traditionally made from the trunks of hollow trees and covered with stretched rawhide. The drums are used at the pueblo's ceremonies, including the **Corn Dance** on July 14. Cochiti artists are also famous for their clay storyteller figures. Many residents specialize in these figurines of children listening to the elders.

On land leased by the pueblo to the Corps of Engineers, you'll find a recreation area with swimming, boating, windsurfing, and especially good fishing. Trout, bass, and northern pike are plentiful.

Admission to the pueblo is free, but remember, no photography, sketching, or recording is permitted. Should you attend the Corn Dance, don't applaud at dances or talk to the participants. (The dances are religious ceremonies.) For more information, call 505-465-2244.

The **Santa Domingo Pueblo**, nine miles south, also holds a ceremonial Corn Dance in early August, with hundreds of participants. The Indians of this pueblo make superb *heishe* beads of turquoise and other stones. The **Church of Santo Domingo** dates to 1886. Visitors are welcome daily from 8am until an hour before sunset, but again, photography is not allowed.

DEMING

Near the Mexican border, Deming celebrates several annual events, including the **Rockhound Roundup** in March. Collectors find abundant agate, fire opal, and jasper in the Little Florida Mountains south of town. At **Rockhound State Park**, off SR 11, rock hunters can find all sorts of semi-precious stones, even amethyst-filled geodes. There's a small admission charge to the park for each carload of people, but anything you find is yours to keep free. The park is open daily 8am-5pm (phone 505-546-6812).

An interesting museum of settler memorabilia, the **Deming Luna Mimbres Museum** (301 S. Silver St., phone 505-546-2382) displays a Mimbres Indian exhibit with baskets and pottery, pioneer clothing, military hardware, a quilt room, and an antique doll collection. There's even a room with a 19th-century funeral home exhibit. The museum's transportation annex has street scenes of long-ago Deming. It's open Mon-Sat 9am-4pm; closed holidays.

Near Deming in the little town of Rodeo, the **Chiricahua Gallery** on Hwy. 80 gives local artists a place to show and sell their work — paintings, photographs, ceramics, quilts, leather, and pottery. The gallery, which also sponsors workshops and classes, is open Tue-Sat 10am-4pm (phone 505-557-2225).

DULCE

The principal town of the Jicarilla Apache Indian Reservation, Dulce offers two fun festivals: the **Little Beaver Roundup** in late July and the **Stone Lake Festival** in mid-September. Dulce's residents are famous for their woven baskets and elaborate crafts. For details, call Tribal Headquarters at 505-759-3242.

ESPAÑOLA

Founded in 1598 by the Spaniards, Española was the first capital of New Mexico. Today, it's a trading and distribution center for the many Indian pueblos that surround it.

The Pojoaque Tribe, nearly wiped out by smallpox in the late 1800's, moved back to the pueblo in the 1930's; there are about 200 members today. The tribe operates the **Poeh Center and Museum**, which features work by their artists. Traditional Indian dances begin at 11am and 1pm on weekends. On the first Saturday in August, the pueblo hosts the **Pojoaque Plaza Fiesta**; arts and crafts and ancestral Indian, western, and international folk dancing are some of the attractions. The tribe's ceremonial dances can be seen each Dec. 12 and on All Kings' Day (Jan. 6). For details, call 505-455-3460.

In the "Valley of the Wild Roses" (*Kha P'o*), the pueblo of **Santa Clara** is known for its fine pottery. If you knock on the doors of houses with "Pottery for Sale" signs, you'll be invited to meet the artists and watch them work. Guided tours of Santa Clara's ancestral dwellings run daily, except on Christmas and the pueblo's feast day, Aug. 12. Make reservations a week in advance for the tours, which can include a traditional Indian meal at a Santa Clara home (phone 505-753-7362). Cameras are allowed by permit only.

Picuris, the smallest of the Tiwa pueblos, was settled in 1200 and now has about 250 members. The pueblo offers tours of a *kiva* and other structures excavated in the 1960's. Artifacts from Picuris's past are displayed in a small museum, open daily from 8am-7pm. Aug. 9 and 10 mark the pueblo's **San Lorenzo Feast Days**, which begin with a sunset dance followed by contests and more dances.

GALLUP

Gallup is best known as the trading center for the Navajo Nation and the Indians of the nearby Zuni Pueblo. Highlighting Gallup's calendar of events is the **Inter-Tribal Indian Ceremonial** — days of dances, games, arts, and crafts, presented by tribes from throughout North America. The ceremonial takes place at Red Rock Park in the second week in August. (From Memorial Day to Labor Day, dancers also perform there daily at 7:30pm.) The park is home to a museum on the Indians' culture, with displays of artwork and crafts. It's open daily 8am-4:30pm.

Nearby **Zuni**, the only surviving settlement of the "Seven Cities of Cibola" sought by Coronado in his quest for gold, preserves ancient Indian rites. The Zuni are master carvers, renowned for their jewelry and animal fetishes. In Zuni, outsiders are permitted to see the famous masked dances—many other pueblos forbid outsiders from these dances — and various ceremonial dances run throughout the year. Visitors are welcome every day from dawn to dusk, but get permission before taking pictures (phone 505-782-4481).

Just out of town on I-40, **Red Rock State Park** boasts a natural 6,500-seat amphitheater at the base of red sandstone cliffs. And **Red Rock Museum** has great displays of Southwestern Indian culture. There are also two nature trails, one of which is wheelchair accessible. The Park is open daily 8am-4:30pm (phone 505-722-3839).

GRANTS

In some ways, California's Gold Rush was no more important than what happened in Cibola County in 1950, when a Navajo rancher named Paddy Martinez discovered an odd, yellow rock. His friends couldn't identify it, so he sent it to the local assayer's office. The rock was uranium, and the boom began. Fortune-seekers with Geiger counters raced to the mesas. When the dust settled, the uranium industry employed more than 5,000, and the population of Grants had tripled.

By 1979, the industry was contributing millions of dollars to the local economy. But after the accident at Three Mile Island, the price of uranium tumbled. Today, fewer than 100 people work in the mining and milling of uranium, and Grants is mainly known for the **El Mal País National Monument**, 376,000 acres of lava beds and ice caves. Within the park are **Anasazi ruins** and **La Ventana**, one of the state's largest natural arches. The ancient **Zuni-Acoma Trail** lets hikers cross four major lava flows. Wear heavy footgear and take extreme care—*el mal país* means "bad country" in Spanish. Remember, too, that the park is an archeological area, and the penalties for disturbing artifacts are severe. The Forest Service has a brochure detailing all the sites in the park. It's available at the visitors center, which is open daily 8am-5pm from Memorial Day to Labor Day weekend (phone 505-285-5406).

Another good brochure comes from the Grants Chamber of Commerce (100 Iron Ave., phone 505-287-4802 or 800-748-2142). Called *Crossroads of Faith*, it describes the seven old missions in the area and their feast days.

HOBBS

The **Lea County Cowboy Hall of Fame and Western Heritage Center** on the New Mexico Junior College campus in Hobbs was founded to honor area residents who were rodeo performers and the pioneer women of nearby ranches. Other exhibits detail the area during the last 150 years. It's open Mon-Fri 10am-5pm, Saturday 1pm-5pm (phone 505-392-1275).

The New Mexico wing of the Confederate Air Force has a display in **The Flying Museum** at the Lea County Airport. The **Thelma Webber Southwest Heritage Room** in the Memorial Library at the College of the Southwest houses artifacts from prehistoric Indians, early settlers, and oil fields. It's open Mon-Fri 8am-5pm in the summer (phone 505-392-6561, ext. 315).

LAS CRUCES

Las Cruces, home to New Mexico State University, hosts a great annual party call the **Whole Enchilada Festival**, held the first weekend in November. You'll find constant entertainment, including street dances, a parade, and a chili cook-off. The festival ends with the cooking of the world's largest enchilada. Information about the celebration and a brochure detailing the city's two historic districts are available at the Convention and Visitors Bureau, 311 N. Downtown Mall, Las Cruces, NM 88001 (phone 505-524-8521).

The **Branigan Cultural Center** on the Downtown Mall displays work by local artists (open Mon-Fri 8am-5pm, phone 505-524-1422). The **Las Cruces Museum of Natural History** (in the Mesilla Valley Mall, 700 S. Telshor Blvd., phone 505-522-3120) has interesting exhibits and includes some live animals. It's open Sun-Thur noon-5pm (open until 9pm on weekends). NMSU's **University Museum** presents exhibits of local interest. It's open Tue-Sat 10am-4pm (phone 505-646-3739).

LAS VEGAS

There are no slot machines or chorus girls in Las Vegas, but it does have more than 900 buildings listed on the National Register of Historic Places, as well as ruts made by thousands of wagon wheels — testament to the area's popularity as a retail center on the old Santa Fe Trail. You can tour ancient adobe buildings in town, as well as Victorian-style structures. Brochures and maps outlining walking tours are available at the Chamber of Commerce, 727 Grand Ave. (phone 505-425-8631 or 800-832-5947).

The **Rough Riders Memorial and City Museum** (725 N. Grand, phone 505-425-8726) commemorates the cavalry unit led by Teddy Roosevelt in the Spanish-American War. The museum, which houses items from regiment members and local relics, is open Mon-Sat 9am-4pm (closed holidays).

The **Las Vegas National Wildlife Refuge**, six miles southeast of town, protects the 9,000-acre home of 300 species, including golden and bald eagles, owls, and hawks. Area bird lists and a brochure outlining a self-guided nature trail are available at the refuge office (open Mon-Fri 8am-4:30pm). The refuge is open daily, sunrise to sunset (phone 505-425-3581).

The **La Cueva National Historic Site**, 25 miles north of Las Vegas on SR 518, was founded by the Romero family in the early 1800's and consists of over 35,000 acres. Built in 1835, the Big House — a *hacienda* that was the first home built in New Mexico — is a two-story structure surrounded by high adobe walls that once provided protection from attacks by the Apache and Comanche Indians. The bell mounted on the side of the house warned La Cueva families of a raid and called them from the fields. The great mill ground flour for the Romeros and their neighbors, and at one time there was a blacksmith shop, stables, and pens for livestock. The **San Rafael Mission Church** has exquisite French Gothic windows, which have been restored by local people, using much of the original wood. The Romeros are said to be buried beneath the altar. In autumn, the site hosts a **Raspberry Roundup**, with fresh raspberries, jam, vinegar, and syrup. The ranch is open from early summer to Dec. 20 (phone 505-387-2900).

LOS ALAMOS

Los Alamos has an explosive history, beginning with the volcanic eruption a million years ago that formed the 40-mile Jeméz Mountain chain. During the last phase of eruptions, the volcano collapsed on itself, creating the spectacular **Valle Grande Caldera**, one of the largest such formations on earth.

The first inhabitants of the area, the Anasazi, built their biggest settlement in present-day **Bandolier National Monument**. The earliest buildings were constructed in 1100, and the tribe flourished until the 1500's. Their descendants live today in the nearby pueblos.

In 1943, the government's Manhattan Project, the atomic bomb research and testing program, assembled America's top scientists to harness the power of the atom and create the world's most powerful weapon — which helped the U.S. and its Allies win World War II. At the **Bradbury Science Museum** at 15th and Central, you can view the first casings of the atomic bomb, along with exhibits on weapons research, nuclear accelerators, energy sources, and life science. It's open Tue-Fri 9am-5pm and Sat-Mon 1pm-5pm (phone 505-667-4444).

The **Los Alamos County Historical Museum** on Central Ave., housed in a stone and log cabin, is dedicated to preserving and interpreting the history of the area through displays on everything from prehistoric cliff dwellers to the atomic bomb. Also on the grounds, there's a Tiwa Indian ruin from the 13th century. Leaflets describing a self-guided tour are available. The museum is open Mon-Sat 10am-4pm and Sun 1pm-4pm (phone 505-662-4493).

The **Fuller Lodge Art Center** (2132 Central Ave., phone 505-662-9331) is in the west wing of a building that once housed the wartime scientists. The center, a visual arts gallery, features art by New Mexico artists and sponsors a regional exhibition each June. It's open Mon-Sat 10am-4pm and Sun 1pm-4pm.

RATON

For centuries, Spanish explorers used Raton Pass through the Rocky Mountains, but the trail was too rough for wagons. In 1866, a mountain man who saw a business opportunity blasted a path through the mountains and set up a toll gate. If the wagons didn't want to pay, he didn't care. They could turn around and detour 100 miles east. Raton grew up around the toll gate, and a railroad bought the toll road in 1879. The town quickly developed as a train, mining, and ranching center for the New Mexico territory.

Downtown Raton is well preserved, with a Victorian atmosphere along **First Street**. The self-guided walking tour of the historic district will send you back in time. The Wells Fargo office, the Santa Fe Depot, the Shuler Theater, and the Palace Hotel still stand.

The quaint **Raton Museum** on First St. is in part of the old Coors Building. Memorable items from the railroad depict life in Raton during the late 19th century. Open Wed-Sat 9am-4pm (phone 505-445-8979).

The National Rifle Association built the **Whittington Center**, a 33,000-acre shooting range ten miles south of town— the most comprehensive such facility in the country. Championship events are held there annually. Plus, there's an unchanged section of the old Santa Fe Trail that cuts through the range. Open daily, dawn to dusk (phone 505-445-3615).

ROSWELL

The **McBride Museum**, at College Blvd. and North Main on the campus of the New Mexico Military Institute, examines the methods of waging war and preserving peace. Exhibits emphasize the participation of the people of New Mexico, as well as the service of the Institute's graduates. Open Tue-Thur 8:30am-3pm (phone 505-624-8220).

The **Roswell Museum and Art Center** (11th and Main, phone 505-624-6744) contains artifacts and art pertaining to Southwestern culture, including paintings by Georgia O'Keefe and Peter Hurd, who was born in Roswell. The Goddard Wing of the Museum features Dr. Robert Goddard's first laboratory, with exhibits on space and rockets. Goddard worked nearby until his death in 1945, and his experiments led to manned space flight. The Museum, which also has a planetarium, is open Mon-Sat 9am-5pm, and 1pm-5pm on Sunday and most holidays (closed Thanksgiving and Christmas).

Roswell also offers a small **zoo** in a 36-acre park, with a playground, a merry-go-round, a miniature train ride, and a children's fishing lake. It's open daily 10am-sunset (closed Christmas). The zoo is free, but the rides cost 25 cents (phone 505-624-6760).

The **Bitter Lake National Wildlife Refuge**, east of town on 24,000 acres, is host to thousands of cranes, roadrunners, and various waterfowl. A brochure describing a self-guided, eight-mile auto tour is available from the refuge, which is open dawn to dusk year-round (phone 505-622-6755).

SANTA FE

The past is ever-present in Santa Fe, a city that three distinct cultures — Indian, Hispanic, and Anglo — have called home. Soldiers from four nations have marched on Santa Fe's twisted streets. All have left their mark on the city — in the architecture, customs, celebrations, and art. Santa Fe sits on the Indian ruins of *Kaupoge* ("place of shell beads near the water"), and anthropologists believe the area's first residents were ancestors of the Pueblo people who settled along the river. Gardeners and construction crews often find room foundations, pottery shards, and even graves of the early inhabitants.

In the 16th century, lured by tales of gold, Coronado led a band of conquistadors across the mountains and established a permanent settlement near San Juan Pueblo. In 1609, the Spanish government built a capital — Santa Fe — for the province of *Nuevo México* for the kingdom of New Spain. The town, now the oldest capital in North America, was centered on a large plaza, with the Palace of the Governors as its focal point. Today, the plaza is the site of the oldest public building in America — and the heart of modern Santa Fe.

Franciscan missionaries tried to convert the Indians to Christianity until 1680, when the pueblos revolted and killed thousands of colonists. The reconquest of New Mexico began in 1692 under de Vargas, who waged a bloody campaign to subdue the Indians. Eventually, an uneasy peace settled over the land. The Spanish and Pueblo peoples slowly became friends, and the exchange of goods and customs led to a different culture.

New Mexico became a U.S. territory in 1850 and the 47th state in 1912. Santa Fe grew into a crossroads, first as the end of the *Camino Real* (the royal highway to Mexico City), later as the final stop on the Santa Fe Trail. During the late 1800's, Anglo traders and European merchants began to arrive, and artists soon discovered the area's brilliant light and subtle hues.

Throughout the region's history of conquest and frontier violence, the city has been the center of culture and civilization. Its multicultural inhabitants left a legacy that makes Santa Fe the most significant historic city in the American West.

The traveler will first note that Santa Fe is a city of museums and churches. The **Cathedral of St. Francis of Assisi**, one block from the Plaza on Cathedral Place, was built in 1859 to serve the Spanish people of Santa Fe. It was the first church between Mexico and St. Louis to be designated a cathedral. Archbishop Lamy, the main character in Willa Cather's *Death Comes for the Archbishop*, is buried beneath the main altar. The Cathedral is open daily, 6am-6pm (phone 505-982-5619).

Three blocks east of the Plaza at 401 Old Santa Fe Trail, the **Mission of San Miguel of Santa Fe** is one of the nation's oldest churches. Begun in 1610 and damaged during the pueblo revolt in 1680, it was rebuilt in 1710. A bell cast in Spain in 1356 is on display, and priceless ornaments and paintings fill the interior. There's a taped presentation, or you can take a tour Mon-Sat 10am-4pm and Sun 1pm-4:30pm; closed on all holy days (phone 505-983-3974).

The **Sanctuario de Guadalupe**, four blocks west of the Plaza at Agua Fria and Guadalupe, is the country's oldest shrine to Our Lady of Guadalupe. There's an oil painting from 1783 by Alzibar above the altar, as well as a meditation chapel, a history room filled with Spanish colonial art, and a garden with plants of the Holy Land. Built in the 18th century, the building stands at the end of the *Camino Real*, which linked Mexico City to Santa Fe. The mission holds mass once a month and is open Mon-Sat 9am-4pm (phone 505-988-2027).

The **oldest house** in Santa Fe is at 215 De Vargas St., three blocks west of the Plaza. The house holds the remains of a Spanish warrior who, according to legend, was killed by two witches in the 1600's. Open Mon-Fri 9:30am-5pm.

Canyon Road has long been a mecca for artists and art lovers. Six blocks south of the Plaza, the winding road is about two miles long and was once an Indian trail to the Pecos pueblos. The galleries and shops along the route make for a marvelous afternoon stroll. **Canyon Road Art Walks**, held on Fridays from late spring to early fall, lead past historic homes and gardens on the narrow, European-style street.

The **Cristo Rey Church** on Canyon Road, considered the largest adobe building in the country, is a classic example of New Mexico Mission architecture of the Spanish period. Parts of the structure date to 1761 (open daily, 6:30am-7pm).

The **Center for Contemporary Arts**, 291 Barcelona Rd., is home to traveling art exhibits, experimental and foreign films, lectures, and workshops. It's open Mon-Fri 10am-4pm and Saturday noon-4pm (phone 505-982-1338).

At the **Wheelwright Museum of the American Indian**, you'll find changing exhibits of traditional and contemporary Indian art and crafts. (704 Camino Lejo, phone 505-982-4636)

Two buildings have unusual architectural features. The **Scottish Rite Temple** on Washington Ave. (three blocks north of the Plaza) is partly a replica of the Alhambra in Granada, Spain. It's open Mon-Fri 9:30am-4pm, closed holidays (phone 505-982-4414). The **State Capitol**, four blocks south of the Plaza on Old Santa Fe Trail, was built in the shape of the Zia sun symbol, the official emblem of New Mexico. It's open Mon-Fri, 8am-5pm (phone 505-986-4589).

The **Pueblo at Tesuque**, eight miles northwest of the city, holds traditional ceremonies, a fiesta, and a dance on Nov. 12th. The pueblo is open daily, 9am-5pm. Admission is free, but there's a $10 fee for photography (phone 505-984-8414).

Near Tesuque, visit the **Shidoni Foundry and Gallery**. Unique metal pieces are cast there and displayed outdoors on several acres. (Bishops Lodge Rd., phone 505-988-8001)

At the **San Ildefonso Pueblo**, 22 miles northwest of Santa Fe on NM 502, many artists open their homes to people browsing for the highly polished black pottery that is the pueblo's source of renown. There's a small museum with a display of San Ildefonso pots and a visitors center (open 8am-4pm daily, except during ceremonies). San Ildefonso also has a fishing pond and several picnic areas; you must ask for a permit first. Residents perform an animal dance at dawn on Jan. 23, with more dances throughout the day. Cameras are not permitted at the dawn dance or at Easter, but permits are available at other times for photographing, sketching, and recording.

Numerous free events occur in and around the Plaza throughout the year. The oldest is the **Fiesta de Santa Fe** in September, held annually for nearly 275 years. Featuring fireworks, dancing, arts, and crafts, the Fiesta begins with a sunrise mass at Rosario Chapel and ends with a candlelight procession. In between, there's considerable pageantry as the queen, her court, Don Diego de Vargas, and his soldiers preside over the activities on the Plaza. Don't miss the burning of

Zozobra (Old Man Gloom) at Marcy Park—when all worries go up in smoke as the effigy bellows and moans before meeting a fiery death—or the Hysterical Historical Parade, with dancers and marching bands.

On the last weekend in July, the **Spanish Market** offers Spanish-style arts and crafts. To qualify for the show, work must be handmade in the traditional style with materials native to the area. You'll find the finest examples of embroidery, textiles, forged iron, and precious metals at the market. In late August, Santa Fe's internationally famous **Indian Market** hosts over 800 Indian artists and thousands of visitors.

Christmas in Santa Fe brings **Las Posadas**, a reenactment of Mary and Joseph's search for a room on Christmas Eve. The city fills with *farolitos* and *luminerias*, and some streets are blocked for pedestrians to walk and enjoy the magical light.

Just north of the Santa Fe Plaza, the **Seña Plaza** is one of the most beautiful and secluded historic sites in Santa Fe. Once the central court of a large hacienda, the plaza has been transformed into an intimate garden.

In recent years, Santa Fe has become a center of holistic health practitioners and New Age philosophers. In addition to the New Age stores and alternative therapists, there are over 200 art galleries and hundreds of unique boutiques. One of the most fun things to do in Santa Fe is window-shop. Just walk in any direction from the Plaza.

SILVER CITY

Though Silver City began with the discovery of silver in the late 1860's, it was never the typical boom-and-bust town. By 1872, it was the county seat of Grant County and soon became the supply center for nearby mining camps. In its early years, the area attracted many legendary figures—Kit Carson, William Randolph Hearst, Roy Bean, and Billy the Kid. Today, copper mining and processing provides the major source of income for the town.

The **Silver City Museum** (312 W. Broadway, phone 505-538-5921; open 9am-4pm Tue-Fri, 10am-4pm Sat and Sun) is located in the **Ailman House**, built in 1881. One of many Victorian buildings in town made from local brick, the house exudes an opulence that reflects the optimism of the mining-boom era. Exhibits in the museum explore the history of the Southwest through a collection of frontier memorabilia, archeological artifacts, Southwestern Indian pottery, and objects from Tyrone, an early mining town. Extensive files and photo archives are available to researchers. Outside, there's a landscaped courtyard and a demonstration garden of native plants. Special events at the museum include the annual New Mexico Cowboy Poetry Gathering in August, a Victorian Christmas Evening, and the Fourth of July Ice Cream Social.

The **Western New Mexico University Museum** in Fleming Hall houses the largest collection of prehistoric Mimbres pottery in the country. Also on display: pottery from the Casa Grande ruins, stone tools, and jewelry. It's open Mon-Fri 9am-4pm (phone 505-538-6386).

Piños Altos, six miles north of Silver City on the Continental Divide, was a camp for miners in the late 1800's. Its small population, many descended from the town's founders, have maintained the Old West atmosphere of the tiny town. The **Piños Altos Historical Museum**, housed in a circa-1860 log cabin, preserves items from the town's mining era. You'll also enjoy touring the dirt streets and buildings dating from the days when a miner was worth $1.20 per day. The Buckhorn Saloon and Opera House, Tyrone Mercantile, Hearst's Church, and the Old Fort and Trading Post have all been restored. The **Santa Rita del Cobre Fort**, built in 1802 for protection from the Apaches, was on the site of the present-day Kennecott Copper Mine. The **Methodist Episcopal Church**, an adobe building with stained glass windows, which once claimed William Randolph Hearst's mother as a principal benefactor, now sponsors art shows and exhibits. The **Mercantile Building**, one of the first retail establishments in the county, initially supplied miners and U.S. Cavalry scouting parties. Today, it's an ice cream parlor and soda shop, where you can see relics of the old Post Office, an ornate coal-burning stove, and the cash register used since 1916.

The Gila Gateway Station has displays on the **Gila Wilderness and National Forest**, which encompasses about three million acres; the main unit is close to Silver City. These canyons and mountain ranges were the stronghold of the Apache warrior Geronimo. The **Catwalk** was built in 1897, after the Apaches were no longer a threat. Engineers installed a pipe to supply water to a mill whose foundations still cling to the canyon wall. The men who walked the pipeline called it the "catwalk," and today visitors can stroll along the cool canyon and enjoy hiking and picnicking.

About 45 miles north of Silver City, the **Gila Cliff Dwellings National Monument** displays seven natural openings on the face of the cliff; in five of them, there are 42 rooms built in the 13th century by the Mogollon people. You can take a self-guided tour of the monument (a one-mile loop trail begins at the parking area). The visitors center, two miles from the entrance on SR 15, has exhibits about the dwellings (open daily 8am-4:30pm, phone 505-536-9461). You might also enjoy driving the 110-mile scenic route, with overlooks that give sweeping views and a perspective on the magnitude of the cliffs and the vast country. The cliff dwellings are open daily from 8am-6pm from Memorial Day to Labor Day and from 9am-4pm the rest of the year.

Near Silver City, on a mesa overlooking a Phelps Dodge open-pit mine, a rock pinnacle called **The Kneeling Nun** has been a landmark for centuries for Indians, pioneers, wagon trains, and prospectors.

Annual events in Silver City include April's **Gila Bird and Nature Festival**, with bird tours, nature walks, and archeology tours. July's **Frontier Days** feature crafts, entertainment, dancing, and townspeople dressed in mining-era costumes. **Mining Days** runs in September, with a barbecue, mock shoot-outs, a chili cook-off, and mining contests. Another fun event, the **Cielo Kite Festival**, occurs in October.

The Silver City/Grant County Chamber of Commerce (1103 N. Hudson, Silver City, NM 88061; phone 505-538-3785 or 800-548-9378) has a wonderful publication that details four historic and scenic tours out of Silver City. The first goes to Piños Altos. The second is a "Billy the Kid tour," featuring his early days, his mother's grave, and recollections of the sheriff and Billy's friends. Tour three takes you to the cliff dwellings, and tour four relates the Mogollon story.

SOCORRO

In Spanish, *socorro* means "help" or "aid." In 1598, weary explorers from the Juan de Onate expedition gave the name to the site after the Indians there offered them badly needed shelter and food. The Socorro grant was a four-square league (2.7 miles), measured from the altar of the church. The first settlers arrived in 1836, and by 1889, the New Mexico School of Mines was established. A division of the school boasts a **Mineral Museum**, which holds one of the most complete collections in the state, plus an exhibit of fossils. The museum is open Mon-Fri 8am-5pm (phone 505-835-5420).

The park area of Socorro's Plaza was established in the 1800's; the park and gazebo today evoke bygone days. The **Old San Miguel Mission**, north of the Plaza at 403 Camino Real, was built in 1615 with massive adobe walls and huge carved *vigas*. General Manuel Armijo, the last governor under the Mexican regime, is buried beneath the church, along with other prominent residents of long ago. The church is open for prayer (or just looking) during the day. Some artifacts are displayed in the church office (phone 505-835-1620).

The **Val Verde Hotel**, a registered historic landmark, was built in 1912, when it proudly boasted all the modern conveniences — such as hot and cold running water.

Magdalena, 25 miles west of Socorro, was the end of the trail for the big cattle drives. At one time, more cattle were shipped from Magdalena than from any place in the country. In town, the old Santa Fe Railroad Depot has been preserved and is now the town's City Hall. The Catholic church has also been restored, and each year it holds memorial services for the miners of **Kelly**, a nearby ghost town. As you drive into Kelly, you can see the profile of Mary Magdalene on the side of

Twenty-seven dishes comprise the Very Large Array.

Magdalena Mountain. According to legend, if you could get to Magdalena Mountain where Mary's face was visible, you would be safe from Indian attack.

The **Bosque del Apache National Wildlife Refuge**, 18 miles south of town on NM 1, is open to the public a half-hour before sunrise to a half-hour after sunset. During migration periods, the 58,000-acre refuge becomes a birdwatcher's paradise. You may even catch a glimpse of the rare whooping crane. In addition, over 400 mammals, reptiles, and amphibians are protected within the park. You can drive through the refuge on a 15-mile loop or hike a 3/4-mile trail through the marsh. The park hosts the **Festival of the Cranes** each November. For details, call the refuge at 505-835-1828.

You can't miss the **Very Large Array Radio Telescope** (VLA), about 50 miles west of town off US 60. The group of 27 dishes collects radio waves from space to "photograph" the heavens. The visitors center has displays that describe radio astronomy and the telescope, and you can see the antennas on a self-guided walking tour. The center is open year-round from 8:30am-sunset (phone 835-7000).

Socorro's Chamber of Commerce is located at 103 Francisco de Avondo, Socorro, NM 87801 (phone 505-835-0424).

TAOS

Combining aspects of the Wild West, magnificent scenery, and Southwestern art and culture, Taos is truly a special place. Indians first occupied this region; conquistadors, fur traders, and miners followed. Three cultures represent the three villages that make up Taos: the original Spanish town, now the center of art and tourism; Taos Pueblo, home of the Taos Indians; and Rancho de Taos, a community famous for its mission church, one of the most photographed sites in New Mexico.

The mission was founded in 1598, but in 1680, the Indians united to drive out the Spanish, and the Taos Pueblo began. However, the Spanish legacy remains visible throughout the area. The 200-year-old **Taos Plaza**, still in its original shape, forms the heart of the shopping district. The Rancho de Taos Plaza centers around one of the Southwest's most splendid buildings, the **San Francisco de Asis Church**, made famous by the paintings of Georgia O'Keefe. Built in 1710, St. Francis contains beautiful examples of Spanish religious carvings, including two altarpieces that date to the founding of the church. The rectory houses an Henri Ault painting, *The Shadow of the Cross*, which depicts Christ carrying a cross — sometimes. Each October 4th, a candlelight procession honors St. Francis. The church is open Mon-Sat 9am-4pm (phone 505-758-2754).

Kit Carson, the legendary scout, is buried at **Kit Carson State Park**, two blocks north of the Plaza. The other grave sites in the park form a remarkable directory of Taos's history. The park is open daily 8am-5pm (phone 505-758-4160).

Taos is perhaps best known as an artists' community. The **Harwood Foundation Museum** features paintings, drawings, sculpture, and photographs by Taos artists from 1898 to the present, plus Spanish folk art, including over 80 *retablos*. The

Harwood also houses the Taos Public Library, which includes a collection of D.H. Lawrence's works and the Padre Martinez collections. The museum, at 238 Ledoux St., is open Mon-Fri noon-5pm and Saturday 10am-4pm (phone 505-758-9826).

The **Stables Art Center**, at 133 Paseo del Pueblo, hosts changing exhibits by local artists. Each exhibit lasts for six weeks. It's open Mon-Sat 10am-5pm and Sunday noon-5pm (phone 505-758-2036).

The **Firehouse Art Collection**, at the corner of Civic Plaza Drive and Placitas Road, holds over 100 works of art by the great Taos pioneers and contemporary artists. All work is donated to support the efforts of Taos firefighters (open Mon-Fri 10am-4pm; phone 505-758-3386).

The **Taos Plaza**, in the heart of Taos, flies the American flag day and night, as permitted by a special act of Congress after Kit Carson and his friends guarded the flag to protect it from Confederate sympathizers during the Civil War. On the south side of the Plaza, the **La Fonda Hotel** contains an exhibit of D.H. Lawrence's paintings that were once banned in London. **La Loma Plaza**, a natural fortification built in the late 18th century to protect farmers from the Indians, is now part of the historic district. **Taos Historic Walks**, 1.5-hour guided walking tours, leave regularly from the Kit Carson complex from June to October.

For nearly 1,000 years, the Taos Indians have lived at or near the **Taos Pueblo**, two miles north of town. The largest multi-storied pueblo structure in the U.S., the Pueblo maintains a way of life little changed by either modernity or 400 years of Spanish and Anglo presence. Because it's a National Historic Monument, the members of the Pueblo who still live in the old village go without electricity and modern plumbing. The Pueblo's artisans produce beautiful wares using techniques handed down through the generations. Mica-flecked pottery, silver and turquoise jewelry, and tanned buckskin moccasins and drums are characterized by the timeless designs.

The annual festivals in Taos maintain the area's artistic bent. From January-March, the **Art Trek** features area artists present-

Taos Pueblo (photo: Don Laine)

ing music, dance, and readings on Saturday from 4pm to 7pm. In mid-January, the **Winter Wine Festival** offers tastings, seminars, and gourmet dinners (some of which charge a fee), and in late January, the **Winter Carnival** offers horse-drawn sleigh rides, dog sled contests, and snowmobile races. The **Spring Arts Festival** highlights mid-May through June with theater, concerts, and art. The **Fall Arts Festival** in early October includes gallery openings, an arts and crafts fair, and an opportunity to meet the many artists who make Taos their home.

Eight miles northwest of Taos on US 64, one of the highest bridges in the nation spans the **Río Grande Gorge**. Nearby, the **Carson National Forest** encompasses over a million acres, including Wheeler Peak, the highest point in the state (13,161 feet). The **Enchanted Circle Scenic Highway**, an 84-mile loop, offers a panoramic view of the southern Rocky Mountains. In addition to black bears, mountain lions, and bighorn sheep, the Carson National Forest has 400 miles of mountain streams, many stocked with trout, and over 300 miles of trails. Many summer hiking trails become cross-country ski trails in the winter. Trail guides are available at any park office. The Forest Supervisor can be reached at Box 558, Taos, NM 87571 (phone 505-758-6200).

The ruins of the **Mission San Geronimo de Taos** are near the entrance to the Pueblo, and **San Geronimo Feast Days** (Sept. 29-30) begin with a sundown dance and vespers at the church. The next day features contests, traditional dancing, and an arts and crafts fair. The second week in July brings the **Taos Pueblo Powwow**, with over 40 tribes from across North America gathered for two days of dancing. A **Corn Dance** is held in June, the **Procession of the Virgin** on Christmas Eve.

Guided tours of the Pueblo are available May through October, and visitors are welcome daily from 8am-5pm year-round. Cameras are not allowed at ceremonies.

The Chamber of Commerce is located at 1139 Paseo del Pueblo Sur, Taos, NM 87571 (phone 505-758-3873 or 800-732-8267).

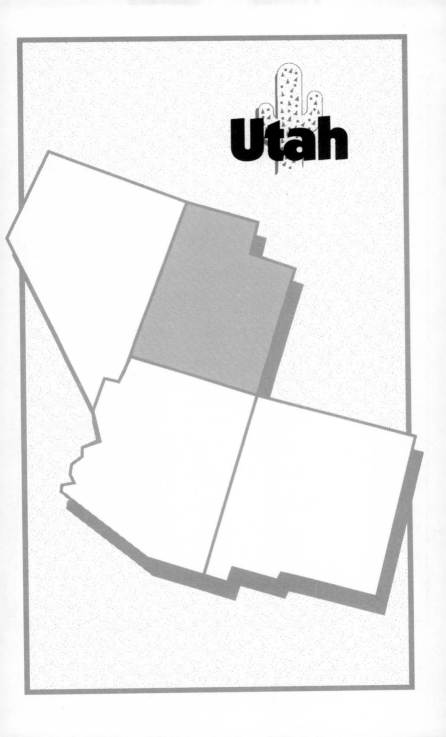

Utah

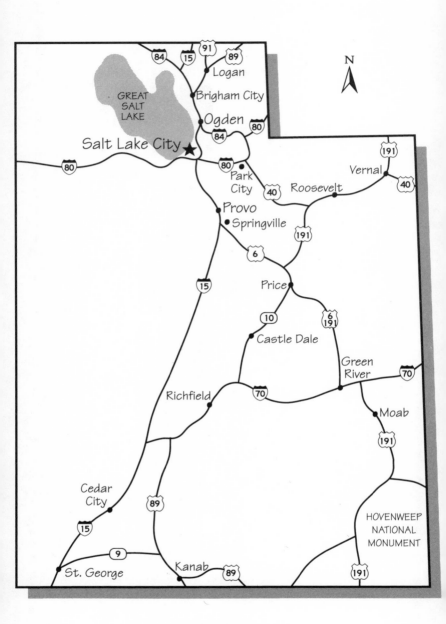

UTAH

Utah

Imagine a land of rugged canyons, trout-filled lakes, majestic rivers, ancient rock art, an inland sea, five national parks, and six national monuments. It's all in Utah, and you won't be able to resist its charms. At certain moments — when the waxing moon rises above the canyons, or when the setting sun blazes off snow-capped peaks, or when the clouds turn purple after a rain — just watching the Utah sky becomes a spectator sport.

Observed from the mountains in the evening, Salt Lake City, the state's largest population center, is a quiet pool of light. You'll understand why the city's founder, Brigham Young, declared, "This is the place!" when he first saw the valley. Salt Lake City has always lured and delighted visitors. Filled with historic homes, and buildings. it has become a major destination for vacationers and business travelers. The city enjoys a spectacular setting at the foot of the Wasatch Mountains, with the Great Salt Lake visible on one side and the Great Salt Lake Desert on the other. In this area, the Mormons chose to settle, the Golden Spike marked the end of the first transcontinental railroad, and early trappers thought they had discovered an arm of the Pacific when they first saw the Great Salt Lake.

Though Utah is known for its Mormon community, the state's largest immigrant group was Greek, especially in Park

City. Near the town of Price, in the center of Castle Country, you'll see evidence of much earlier settlement, with cave dwellings and petroglyphs.

Natural splendor abounds. The Green River displays multiple personalities, raging through sandstone canyons and slipping past lush meadows, demanding awe one moment and inspiring daydreams the next. The Rainbow Bridge National Monument, one of the seven natural wonders of the world, is considered a sacred place by the Navajo Indians. Moab was familiar territory to Butch Cassidy and the Sundance Kid. Zane Grey used it as the setting for many of his novels, and it's a favorite spot for movie-making today. The Flaming Gorge area is a wonderland of red rocks and spires. Zion National Park is a showplace in every season.

Cedar City makes an ideal headquarters for a visit to southern Utah. You can spend the day exploring old movie sets and ghost towns or hiking through the forests of ponderosa pine, spruce, fir, and aspen in Bryce Canyon. When you reach the overlook, you'll see one of the most remarkable sights in the world: multicolored pinnacles and spires that create a fantasy land whose beauty changes with the time of day. Glen Canyon, another marvelous gorge, was once a maze of valleys cut by the Colorado River. Now it holds Lake Powell, which boasts one of the most dramatic shorelines in the country.

In Cedar Breaks National Monument, the sheer cliffs meld from orange to white at the top, then dissolve into deep rose and coral at the bottom. Thick forests and high meadows make the area ideal for hikers and picnics. In the winter, Cedar Breaks becomes even more spectacular with its blanket of snow.

On Logan's historic Main Street, you'll see churches, banks, and even a "tithing office." Springville, home to the oldest and most beautiful art museum in the state, hosts a World Folkfest in July, with performers from all over the globe.

The myth persists that Utah's streets are rolled up and its doors are locked at sundown, but it's not true. There's an active nightlife — and much is free. The performing arts are vibrant, the ski resorts are always hopping in the winter, and, yes, you *can* get a drink throughout the state.

BRIGHAM CITY

The center of Utah's farming region, the Brigham City area grows peaches, apricots, and cherries. In the summer, there's a section of highway called the **Golden Spike Fruitway** that's lined with fruit stands. Brigham City celebrates **Peach Days** each year right after Labor Day. The local landmark is **Inspiration Point** near the top of Willard Peak, and on a clear day you can see forever — or at least into Idaho and Nevada.

The **Brigham City Tabernacle**, built in 1876, is notable for its architecture. Guided tours are available daily from 8am-8pm May-October (phone 801-723-5376).

The **Brigham City Museum and Gallery**, at 24 North 300 West St., displays pioneer artifacts and furnishings, plus exhibits by local artists (open Tue-Fri 11am-6pm, Sat 1pm-5pm; phone 801-723-6769).

CASTLE DALE

Eons ago, geologic upheavals formed a giant dome of rock, which collapsed into a broken array of multicolored sandstone. Wind and water carved the jumble into stunning formations — buttes, canyons, pinnacles, and mesas. Today, this area, known as the **San Rafael Swell**, is considered one of the undiscovered natural wonders of the Southwest. This high desert is vastly different from the Sonoran Desert of Arizona. It was also the site of Butch Cassidy's hideout.

The town of Castle Dale was built in 1875 by a cattleman. The local **Emery County Museum** in City Hall contains pioneer and Indian artifacts, plus re-creations of an old law office, a schoolroom, and a general store. Open Mon-Fri 10am-4pm (phone 801-381-2115).

The lobby of the Museum holds an allosaur skeleton from the **Cleveland-Lloyd Dinosaur Quarry**, one of the most productive such sites in the world. Over 70 different animals have been recovered at the Quarry, which was once a muddy lake that trapped plant-eating dinosaurs. Excavations continue at the bone beds, and there's a visitors center with exhibits and a nature trail. Open daily 9am-6pm from Memorial Day to Labor Day (phone 801-637-5060).

From late July to early August, the town offers the colorful and exciting **Castle Valley Historical Pageant**, which portrays the triumphs and tragedies of the first settlers. The pageant begins at dusk, and there's an antique machinery show to go along with it.

CEDAR CITY

An abundance of iron ore brought Scottish and Welsh settlers to the Cedar City area, and the town's **Iron Mission State Park** now preserves the site of the first iron foundry west of the Mississippi. The park's museum has a great collection of horse-drawn vehicles from Utah farms and towns, including a bullet-scarred wagon from Butch Cassidy's time, a Wells Fargo stagecoach, an old milk wagon, and even a one-horse open sleigh. You'll also see over 200 Indian relics, including clothing and weapons used by the Southern Paiutes. The museum is open daily except holidays from 9am-5pm (phone 801-586-9290). A picnic area is available.

The **Braithwaite Fine Arts Gallery** on the campus of Southern Utah State College houses works by national and local artists from the 19th century to the present. Pottery and textiles are also part of the permanent collection. Open Mon-Fri 10am-7:30pm, Saturday and Sunday 1pm-5pm (phone 801-586-5432).

Cedar City proudly hosts the **Utah Shakespearean Festival** from late June through early September. While there is a charge for performances, there are many free events associated with the fair. Costumed vendors wander the streets, and a complimentary **Greenshow** — Elizabethan dancing, madrigal singing, lute playing, and sonnet readings — takes place in the Randall Jones Theatre an hour before each show. You can also take a free backstage tour that explores the theater and its costume, makeup, and scene shops. The tour runs Tue-Sat at 11am and lasts an hour and a half. The festival also sponsors literary seminars Tue-Sun at 9am and 10am and production seminars at 11:30am. The classes are conducted by musicians, costumers, and actors. Babysitting services are available on the festival grounds.

Other annual events in Cedar City include the **Paiute Restoration Gathering** in June, with a powwow, parade, talent night, and softball tournament, and a **Renaissance Faire** in July, which adds to the fun of the Shakespeare Festival. Also in July, activities in the City Park commemorate the arrival of the Mormon pioneers at the **Pioneer Day Celebration**. In November, the **Iron Mission Days** fest involves a fun run, pioneer crafts, and the Birthday Ball. In early December, the **Winterfest and Light Parade** ushers in the holiday season with a week of activities, including a community bonfire.

It's nowhere near the Mason-Dixon Line, but **Dixie National Forest**, east of town, reminded settlers of the South, so that's how it got its name. Protecting almost two million acres, Dixie is Utah's largest forest. A three-hour tour of the park leaves Tue-Sat at 9am and 1pm from Ruby's Inn near Bryce Canyon; rangers describe recreational opportunities and the wildlife in the forest. Nine miles southeast of Cedar City and within Dixie, the **Markagunt Plateau** also offers many recreational facilities. Nearby **Brian Head Peak**, **Strawberry Point**, and **Zion Overlook** provide spectacular views. You'll also find bristlecone pine trees, one of the oldest living things on earth, on a self-guided trail at **Midway Summit**. In the heart of the forest, **Pine Valley Mountain** towers nearly 11,000 feet above sea level. The dome, formed by a build-up of volcanic ash over centuries, is the largest of its kind in the world. Dixie maintains a network of hiking and horseback trails. For more information, stop by the Duck Creek Visitors Center (open daily 10am-5pm from Memorial Day to Labor Day).

The Iron County Tourism Bureau is at 286 North Main, Cedar City, UT 84720 (phone 801-586-4484).

DELTA

The **Great Basin Museum**, one block north of US 50 at 328 W. 100 North, features an exhibit about the Topaz Relocation Center, an internment camp for Japanese-Americans during World War II. There's also an 1893 steam-engine tractor, arrowheads, fossils, and pioneer artifacts. Open Mon-Sat 10am-4pm (phone 801-864-5013).

GOULDINGS

A re-creation of a 1920's trading post fills the entire first floor of the **Gouldings Monument Valley Museum**, two miles west of US 163 at Gouldings Lodge. There are also displays of memorabilia from films made in the area and the Goulding family's personal artifacts. Open daily 11am-8pm from April to December (phone 801-727-3225).

GREEN RIVER

Your first stop in Green River should be the **John Wesley Powell River History Museum**, which really captures the thrill of the West's wild rivers. It houses fascinating replicas of the boats used by explorers, including a unique round hull used by Indians and the crude rafts of early river runners. The museum also has an exciting film on the history of river exploration and a River Runner's Hall of Fame, which commemorates a variety of brave people. The museum, at 885 East Main, is open daily 8am-8pm (phone 801-564-3427).

The first farming community built and settled by non-Mormons, Green River is known for its watermelons, so the town celebrates **Melon Days** in mid-September with free watermelon for everyone.

Green River State Park, nestled beneath towering cottonwood trees, features a campground and picnic area. A variety of trees and small wildlife add to the setting, and slide shows are presented in the evening in summer.

Just five miles east of town, the **Crystal Geyser**, a cold water geyser, erupts on an irregular basis three or four times a day.

The powerful spray reaches 100 feet. You might also see wild herds of goats roaming the area.

HELPER

Settled in 1870 by a coal prospector, Helper offers the **Western Mining and Railroad Museum** at 296 South Main in the town's historic district. The museum displays artifacts relating to the area's railroad and mining operations, including 19th-century mining tools, railroad equipment, the wooden steps from which Butch Cassidy robbed the Pleasant Valley Coal Company, and WPA artwork from the Depression. You'll also find two outdoor display areas with mining equipment and a circa-1917 caboose from the railroad. Open Mon-Sat 9am-5pm from May to September, Tue-Sat 11am-4pm from Oct to April (phone 801-472-3009).

HOVENWEEP NATIONAL MONUMENT

Hovenweep is an Indian word meaning "deserted valley." The tumbled piles of stonework — the remains of pueblos and cliff dwellings — testify to the large population that once lived in the valley. Those early inhabitants were part of the large group of Pueblo Indians who lived in the Four Corners region for centuries. Something forced them to abandon their homes sometime before 1300, and they moved south, never to return. The monument consists of six separate groups of ruins, all noted for their square and oval towers. The National Monument Headquarters is at the Square Tower group in Utah, where you'll find a ranger station and a campground. A ranger is on duty all year. Phone 303-529-4461 for details.

The nearby town of **Mexican Hat** was named for a huge boulder which resembles a sombrero that's 60-feet wide and 12-feet thick. The formation balances atop a cliff that can be seen from the road. **Gooseneck State Reserve** off SR 261 provides an overlook into the twisting canyon below. At one point, the river makes a three-mile curve around a ridge that's only 100 yards wide.

KANAB

In a spectacularly scenic region south of Bryce Canyon, Kanab was once a fort, built as a defense against the Indians. Hundreds of movies have been filmed in the area. One especially popular site is a typically western "Main Street" in **Old Paria**, six miles east of the village. Also, be sure to see **Coral Pink Sand Dunes State Park**, a wind-swept wonderland of colored dunes 23 miles northeast of town. Camping is permitted (phone 801-874-2408).

In Kanab, **Heritage House**, at 100 South Main, was built in 1894 by one of the town's first settlers. The Victorian-style house shows an ingenious use of local resources: rocks from the red ledges north of town, local lumber, and locally fired bricks. Inside, there are displays of memorabilia from the time of the original residents. It's open Mon-Sat 9am-5pm (phone 801-644-2542).

A brochure that details a walking tour of 12 historic homes, as well as the Heritage House, is available at the City Office at 40 East 100 North St. (phone 801-644-2534).

LOGAN

As the home of Utah State University, Logan hosts many free events throughout the year. Perhaps the best known is the **Festival of the American West**, which runs from late July to early August. For eight days, visitors can set their clocks back 100 years as they experience the area's lifestyle in the 19th century. Crafts, entertainment, and staged spectacles abound; the smell of food cooking over an open fire fills the air. In addition, **outdoor concerts** run every other Sunday on the patio of Taggart Center on the campus.

Logan has two good museums. The **Daughters of Utah Pioneers Museum**, at 160 N. Main (phone 801-752-5139), features settlers' artifacts and exhibits on the pioneer days. It's open Tue-Fri 10am-4pm from June to August. The **Nora Eccles Harrison Museum of Art**, on the USU campus, focuses on 20th-century American art, with new exhibits every six to eight weeks. It's open Mon-Fri 10am-4pm (phone 801-797-0163).

If you'd like to learn more about the **Main Street Historical District**, there's a brochure available around town that discusses the Cache Knitting Works, the Capitol Theater, and the County Courthouse. The chief monument to the city's past, the **Mormon Temple**, was finished in 1884 and remains one of the state's finest temples. Also in town, the **LDS Tabernacle** was recently renovated to revive its original interior and colors. A good example of the early Mormon meeting houses, the building has served as both a house of worship and a public meeting place. The pipe organ has been described as one of the most beautiful instruments in the state.

For cheese lovers, the **Cache Valley Cheese Chalet**, a cheese factory in nearby Amalga, is open 8am-5pm Mon-Sat (phone 801-563-3281), and the **Gossner Foods Cheese Factory** at 1000 West 1000 North in Logan lets visitors peek at the production process and try free samples. It's open 8am-5:30pm Mon-Sat (phone 801-752-9365).

Logan has a delightful small zoo, **Willow Park Zoo**, with a wandering stream, ponds, and a picnic area nearby. It's open 8am-dusk daily except Christmas, Easter, and New Year's Day (phone 801-750-9893).

The Logan area is famous for its **Jardine Juniper**, believed to be the earth's largest and oldest (over 3,000 years old) juniper tree. An easy five-mile trail up Logan Canyon leads to the tree. **Hardware Ranch**, 25 miles southeast of town, is an elk feeding station where you can learn about elk management and ranch history. In the winter, the ranch offers a 20-minute sleigh ride for a small fee (phone 801-245-3131).

MOAB

The setting for many of Butch Cassidy's escapades and Zane Grey's novels, Moab provides unlimited opportunity for recreation—whitewater rafting, hiking, bicycling, hunting, fishing, boating, and more.

The monumental red spires of **Fisher Tower**, 24 miles northeast of town off SR 128, are probably the most popular outdoor destination. This area is used in many movies and TV commercials (you've seen cars perched on top), and you can get a closer look by hiking two miles from the rest area at the end of the road. Also popular, the **Lasal Mountain Loop Road** winds through Castle Valley and into the mountains. "The Canyon's Edge," a multimedia show presented nightly at the visitors center, explores the natural history of the Colorado Plateau (phone 801-259-7750).

In town, the **Dan O'Laurie Memorial Museum** displays the geology and mineralogy of southeastern Utah. It's open Mon-Sat 1pm-5pm and 7pm-9pm (phone 801-259-7985).

In early June, the **Butch Cassidy Days** celebration features a parade, a rodeo, and live music throughout town. Phone 801-259-8825 for details.

For more information about the wealth of recreation in the area, contact the Moab Visitors Center, 805 N. Main, Moab, UT 84532 (toll free 800-635-6622).

OGDEN

Best known as the site of the Golden Spike, which united the continent by railroad, Ogden was named for a fur trapper and designed by Brigham Young. It's an especially lovely town, with streets lined with poplar and elm trees. The **municipal park** contains five acres of gardens, paths lit with gas lanterns, and picnic areas. Every year during the holidays, the park sponsors Santa's Village and an international Christmas display.

At the **Ogden Tabernacle and Temple**, 2133 Washington Blvd., guided tours of the grounds run daily from 9am to 9pm.

You can see the clothes and furnishings of pioneers at the **Daughters of Utah Pioneers Museum and the Miles Goodyear Cabin**, at 2148 Grant Ave. (phone 801-621-5224). The cabin, built in 1841, is said to be the oldest homestead in Utah. The site is open Mon-Sat 10am-5pm, May-September.

The **Eccles Community Center** displays works by Utah artists (2580 Jefferson Ave., phone 801-392-6935), and the **Museum of Natural Science** at Weber State exhibits dinosaur fossils and geological specimens. Open Mon-Fri 8am-5pm during the school year (phone 801-626-6653).

At the Hill Air Force Base, the **Aerospace Museum** displays aircraft, missiles, and other military hardware in huge indoor and outdoor exhibits. There's a B-29 Super Fortress, a C-119 Flying Boxcar, and a film about the history of the base. Open Tue-Thur 9am-4:30pm (phone 801-777-6868).

Each January, the **Ogden/Hof Sister City Festival and Winterfest** celebrates the long relationship between Ogden and Hof, Germany. Polkas, a torchlight parade, snow-sculpting contests, and a variety of winter sports are all part of the festivities. Call 801-629-8242 for more details.

Information on the area is available from the Ogden Convention and Visitors Bureau, 2501 Wall Ave., Ogden, UT 84401 (phone 801-627-8288).

PARK CITY

Silver was the catalyst for the settlement of Park City. In 1872, a trio of prospectors tapped into a rich vein in Ontario Canyon. Soon, adventurers from around the world flocked to the area, turning the tiny camp into a boomtown. Park City was one of the few Utah towns established by non-Mormons, and during the mining boom, there were 27 saloons on Main Street. When silver prices fell in the 1930's, the town had some hard times, but soon the sport of skiing caught on, and a new boom began. Today, the city is home to the U.S. Ski Team and hosts numerous winter events, including the **Snow Sculpture Winterfest** in February and **Music in the Mountains** in March.

The **Visitor Information Center/Museum**, at 528 Main St., has exhibits explaining Park City's beginnings as a mining town and its transition into a resort. The museum was once the City Hall and is listed on the National Register of Historic Places. Utah's Territorial Jail, used longer than any other hoosegow in the Southwest, remains intact in the basement. The Museum is open Mon-Sat 10am-7pm and Sunday noon-6pm (phone 801-649-6104).

At the **Kimball Art Center** (Park and Main Sts.), the Art Walk and Photo Alley offer artwork from all over the world, plus arts and crafts shops. It's open Mon-Sat 10am-6pm and Sunday noon-6pm (phone 801-649-8882).

Though Park City is best known as a winter resort, its summer is filled with events. The hills resonate during the **Music in the Mountains** performances scheduled throughout the season. In June, the **Savor the Summit** festival offers a variety of great food, plus cooking demonstrations, contests, and music. From mid-June to August, the **Pocket Plaza Entertainment Series** presents a variety of live music every Saturday on Main St. from 1pm-4pm. **Miners Day** in early September offers fun, food, and festivities, with a parade, competitions, and a volleyball tournament. There's also a spectacular **Balloon Festival** in September.

Information and a map for a walking tour through the historic district are available at the Park City Chamber of Commerce, 1910 Prospector Dr. #103, Park City, UT 84060 (phone 801-649-6100).

PRICE

One of the most interesting museums in the Southwest, the **College of Eastern Utah Prehistoric Museum** exhibits Anasazi Indian artifacts, including a collection of figures believed to be 900 years old. The museum also has minerals, fossils, and a Hall of Dinosaurs. They will provide you with information on Indian petroglyphs and tours to the dinosaur quarry nearby. It's open daily 9am-6pm April-Sept (phone 801-637-5060).

Nine Mile Canyon, an outdoor museum close to Price, is a must-see in Utah. Relatively untouched by tourism, the canyon has some remarkable Indian art and remnants of dwellings unspoiled by the centuries. *National Geographic* has featured the extraordinary rock art, which comes in two varieties: pictographs and petroglyphs. Pictographs — designs painted using color found naturally in minerals — are usually destroyed by the weather. They remain in this canyon because so many were painted under ledges or in caves. Petroglyphs are designs cut into the rock, usually in an area where the natural patina of the rock has made the surface darker than the surrounding rock. The art in Nine Mile Canyon depicts animals and humans wearing necklaces, earrings, and headdresses.

You'll quickly become proficient at spotting outcroppings of carvings in the canyon. Some are accessible on foot; others are best viewed through binoculars. There are no services of any kind at the Canyon, so take plenty of water and a picnic, and be sure your car is filled with gas. Although it's called Nine Mile Canyon, the road through the canyon is 50 miles long. A brochure of a self-guided tour is available from the College of Eastern Utah Prehistoric Museum.

More scenic drives out of Price are described in a brochure available from the Castle Country Travel Council, at 155 East Main St. (phone 801-637-3009). They also have maps on self-guided tours to Indian dwellings and the Little Grand Canyon and a description of a walking tour of National Historic Sites in the city.

One of those sites is the Price Municipal Building, at 200 East Main, which contains the **Price Mural**, commissioned by the WPA in 1938. The artist, Lynn Fausett, a local who studied in Europe and New York, has murals in buildings throughout the nation. The Price Mural, which depicts the history of Carbon County and covers about 800 square feet, shows 82 principal figures and many of the original buildings of the county. A favorite scene shows a Fourth of July celebration in 1911, with horse-drawn floats and a marching band.

The walking tour also leads to the **Moynier House**, built in 1909, and the **Hellenic Orthodox Church**, the oldest Greek church in Utah in continuous use.

Price celebrates **Greek Festival Days** in July, and the town honors its multicultural heritage with **International Days** on the second weekend in August.

PROVO

The railroad came to Provo in 1875, linking it to Salt Lake City, and **Brigham Young University** was established two years later to supply teachers for the Utah public schools. The University, at the base of the Wasatch Mountains, is one of the largest church-related private universities in the nation. The 700-acre campus is dominated by the Centennial Carillon Tower, whose

52 bells ring throughout the day. Guided tours of the campus are given at 11am and 2pm Mon-Fri (phone 801-378-4678).

The campus also offers four interesting museums. The **Bean Life Science Museum** houses extensive collections and exhibits of insects, plants, fish, shells, mammals, and birds for research and educational programs. It's open Mon-Sat 10am-5pm (phone 801-378-5051). The **Earth Science Museum**, at 1683 North Canyon Rd. (phone 801-378-3680), contains one of the most extensive fossil collections in the country, and the **Museum of Peoples and Cultures** (700 North 100 East, phone 801-378-6112) has anthropological artifacts from various world cultures. Items made by the Navajo, Shoshone, and the Mexican Chiapa de Corzo Indians are on display, and special emphasis is given to the Mayas of Central America. It's open Mon-Fri 9am-5pm. Finally, the **Harris Museum of Fine Arts** maintains two galleries of European and 19th-century American art, plus exhibits of pottery, ceramics, and sculpture by faculty members and students. A fascinating exhibit of musical instruments includes a snake charmer's flute from India, a mouth organ from Thailand, and Arabian lutes. The galleries are open 8am-5pm Mon-Fri (phone 801-378-4332).

Another good museum, the **Pioneer Park Museum** at 500 West 500 North, contains collections of Western art and artifacts from early Utah, including original cabins from Fort Utah. Open Mon-Fri 2pm-5pm from June to Aug (phone 801-379-6609).

The **Provo Latter Day Saints Temple** at 2200 North Temple Dr., whose golden spires lie in the shadow of the magnificent mountains, offers an awesome view of 50 miles of Utah's heartland. Tours of the grounds run daily from June to September. (Non-Mormons are not allowed in the Temple.)

Two factory tours can be fun. A tour of the headquarters of **Nu Skin International** (75 West Center, phone 801-345-8687) is available weekdays at 10am, 11am, 2pm, and 3pm. The visitors center has displays illustrating the history of skin care. You can also visit the only integrated steel mill west of the Mississippi, at 10 South Geneva Rd. in nearby Orem. For details about the **Geneva Steel Tour**, call 801-227-9420.

Provo is filled with historic sites. Literature for a self-guided tour of historic buildings is available at the Utah County Visitor Center, 51 University Ave., Suite 111, Provo, UT 84601 (phone 801-370-8393). Three sites stand out: **Academy Square**, used by Brigham Young University students for 83 years (550 North University Ave.); **Fort Utah** on Geneva Rd., with a picnic pavilion and playground; and the **Historic Utah County Courthouse**, built in the 1920's and one of the grandest public buildings in the state (51 University Ave.).

Holiday celebrations in Provo include a **Strawberry Festival** in June and **America's Freedom Festival** in July, with a carnival, a clogging competition, a hot-air balloon rally, and a grand parade. You'll also find free musical events — symphony performances, jazz ensembles, organ concerts, and choir presentations — on a regular basis at the various concert halls on the BYU campus.

Finally, the **Alpine Loop Scenic Backway**, one of Utah's most popular scenic drives, winds for 19 miles around Mt. Timpanogos, with impressive views of and access to the Timpanogos and Lone Peak Wilderness area. There are numerous picnic, camping, and hiking opportunities. The road is open from early summer through mid-autumn.

The Provo Orem Chamber of Commerce is at 51 S. University Ave., Room 215, Provo, UT 84603 (phone 801-379-2555).

RICHFIELD

Did you think the **Big Rock Candy Mountain** was just the name of a song? Surprise! There really is such a place, 24 miles south of tiny Richfield on US 89. It's a rainbow-colored mountain with tinted rock formations, and there are canyons nearby with petroglyphs that predate the birth of Christ.

Fremont Indian State Park has a museum that recounts the history of the Anasazi from 500 A.D. to about 1300. There are also pictographs from a nearby hill and many prehistoric artifacts. It's open daily 9am-5pm (phone 801-527-4631).

ROOSEVELT

All you fishing enthusiasts who wonder where they're biting should stop at the **Whiterocks State Fish Hatchery**, 23 miles east of Roosevelt. This complex supplies brook, cutthroat, rainbow, and brown trout — over a million a year — to many Utah recreation areas. It's open daily 8am-4:30pm (phone 801-353-4855).

Brochures on two self-guided tours — the **Early Frontier Tour** and the **Indian Petroglyph Tour** — are available at the Roosevelt Area Chamber of Commerce, 48 South 200 East (phone 801-722-4598). Each tour takes a full day.

SALT LAKE CITY

Most people believe that the first residents of the Salt Lake Valley were Mormons who arrived in 1847. In fact, the area has been inhabited for at least 10,000 years; Mormons simply started the present-day city. Led by Brigham Young, the founders (143 men, three women, and two children) were the first non-Indians to live in the valley.

The Mormons came in search of a region where they could practice their religion free from persecution. When Brigham Young saw the valley, he exclaimed, "This is the place!" On the day of their arrival, they began tilling the soil and planting crops. Within a few days, they had made plans for the Great Salt Lake City, named for the lake that dominates the desert nearby. Out from the center of the city, which is now Temple Square, blocks were arranged in a grid of 10-acre squares, separated by streets 130-feet wide — "wide enough for a team of four oxen and a covered wagon to turn around." Those streets today give the city a notably spacious feeling.

The California Gold Rush brought miners and fortune-seekers to the area, and soldiers were stationed there during the Civil War. The Mormons prospered by trading with these folks, and when the Golden Spike completed the transcontinental railroad, many people traveled to the state to see the "City of Saints." Some stayed to make a fortune in mining; from the 1860's to the 1920's, hundreds of mines opened in the nearby canyons. In 1896, Utah became the 45th state, and Salt Lake City became its capital.

Begin your visit at **Temple Square**. Construction on the Temple, which holds the laws sacred to the Mormon faith, began in 1853. Built with granite blocks hauled by wagon from nearby Cottonwood Canyon, it took almost 40 years to complete. The visitors center, with tours every few minutes, is open in the summer Mon-Fri 8am-7pm (weekends 10am-4pm) and in the winter Mon-Fri 8am-5pm, Saturday 9am-4pm, closed Sunday. In the Tabernacle, organ recitals are given Mon-Sat at noon and Sunday at 2pm. The sublime Tabernacle Choir rehearses Thursdays at 8pm — an absolute must! Their radio broadcast begins at 9:30am Sunday in the 6,500-seat Tabernacle. The doors open at 8:15am, and you must be seated by 9:15am. The acoustics are extraordinary, and you'll never forget hearing the 320-voice choir in this setting. The Mormon Youth Symphony rehearses Wednesday at 8pm, the Youth Chorus Tuesday at 8pm. You are welcome to attend any or all rehearsals. The Temple Square's winter hours are 9am-9pm, and the summer hours are 8am-10pm. The choir office can be reached at 801-521-2822.

One block east of Temple Square is the **Beehive House**, a beautifully restored home that was the official residence of Brigham Young. Built in 1854, it gets its name from the traditional Mormon symbol of industry. Tours of the house are conducted Mon-Sat 9:30am-4:30pm and Sunday 10am-1pm. The house closes early on all holidays (phone 801-240-2671). Near the house, the 76-foot span of **Eagle Gate** was erected in 1859 as the entrance to Brigham Young's farm. A three-ton statue of an eagle with a wingspan of 20 feet hovers over the arch.

The **Brigham Young Monument** at Main and South Temple Streets has a plaque listing the names of the pioneers who arrived on July 24, 1847.

South Temple Street has a large group of 19th-century buildings, including the **Kearns Mansion**, at 603 East South Temple, now the official residence of the Governor of Utah. Built in 1900, the house boasts 28 rooms, six baths, an all-marble

The ornate interior of the Cathedral of the Madeleine.

kitchen, a bowling alley, and three vaults: one for wine, one for silver, and one for jewelry. Guided tours are available May-December on Tuesday and Thursday from 2pm to 4pm (phone 801-538-1005).

The Mormons aren't the only faith in town. On South Temple at C St., the **First Presbyterian Church** is notable for its red sandstone exterior and stained glass windows (open Mon-Fri 9am-5pm; phone 801-363-3889). The Catholic **Cathedral of the Madeleine**, 331 E. South Temple, was built by the first Bishop of Salt Lake City in 1900. It's a Roman Gothic masterpiece, with leaded stained glass windows from Munich, elaborate art, and three altars made of Utah marble; above each is a painting of Mary Magdalene (open daily 8am-7pm; phone 801-328-8941). Begun in 1870, **St. Mark's Cathedral** (231 E. 100 South St.) was constructed with thick sandstone walls and huge wood beams. The organ, said to be the oldest pipe organ in the state, was built in Scotland in 1857. Tours are available Mon-Fri 10am-4pm (phone 801-322-3400).

Where did you really come from? Who were your ancestors? Were they rich, royal, famous, or obscure? Visitors to Salt Lake can discover the answers at the **Family History Library** (35 North West Temple, west of Temple Square), which has the world's largest collection of genealogical information, with 1.6 million rolls of microfilmed records and 225,000 books. Records includes ship passenger lists, military details, land and probate records, and other research aids. Information dates to 1150, and though the library does not have data on everyone who ever lived, it does have a huge collection of records from much of the world. It's open 7:30am-6pm Monday, 7:30am-10pm Tue-Fri, and 7:30am-5pm Saturday (closed Sunday). Guided tours are offered; call 801-240-3702 for details.

Part of the Salt Palace Complex, the **Salt Lake Art Center** (20 South West Temple) features regional and national exhibits emphasizing contemporary art. A full schedule of classes and lectures is offered, including noon lunch lectures every Wednesday. It's open Mon-Sat 10am-5pm and Sunday 1pm-5pm (phone 801-328-4201). Free tours are available of **Symphony**

Hall, also part of the Complex. The hall boasts one of the finest acoustical environments of any concert hall in the world, and over 12,000 square feet of 24-carat gold leaf adorns the interior. It's open daily, May-Sept (phone 801-533-6407). (Incidentally, the first Salt Palace really was made of salt. The building's exterior was "spray-painted" with rock salt to make it sparkle and was illuminated at night with thousands of electric lights. Built in 1899, it burned in 1910.)

The **LDS Church Office Building**, at 50 East North Temple, is the city's tallest structure. Two observation decks, offering lovely views of the mountains and valley, are available on the 26th floor. The building is open Mon-Fri, with free tours from 9am-4:30pm (phone 801-240-2452).

The **Marmalade District Historic Homes** area — bounded by 300 North St. on the south, Center St. on the east, and Quince St., the district's main street, on the west — got its name from the fruit-bearing plants and trees planted by early residents of the area. It's distinguished from other neighborhoods by steep streets, mature landscaping, and a variety of vintage homes. The Utah Heritage Foundation can provide information on tours of the area (phone 801-533-0858).

The **Utah State Capitol**, at the north end of State St., was built with Utah granite and cost almost $3,000,000 in 1915. Inside, Utah history is dramatized with large canvases and murals, and the domed ceiling depicts sea gulls in flight. Summer hours are 6am-8pm daily; winter hours are 8am-6pm daily. Guided tours begin every half-hour from 10am to 3pm (phone 801-538-3000).

The **Brigham Young Grave**, on 1st Ave. between State and A Streets, marks the resting place of the Mormon founder and several of his family members. The focal point of the small plot is the Mormon Pioneer Memorial Monument, dedicated to the brave folks who crossed the plains to reach the Salt Lake Valley.

The **City and County Building**, at Washington Square between 400 and 500 South on State St., was erected in 1894 and served for 19 years as the Capitol. This historic site, once filled with the camps of pioneers in 1847, has been the scene of carnivals, medicine shows, religious services, and even jousting tournaments. The first peace treaty between the Ute and Shoshone tribes was signed here. The Utah Heritage Foundation conducts tours every Tuesday at noon and Saturday at 10am. The building is open Mon-Fri 8am-5pm (phone 801-533-0858).

Hansen Planetarium (15 South State St.) houses a projector that takes visitors on a trip to the planets four times a day. The Exhibit Hall contains a rotating relief globe of the earth, a large lunar hemisphere, and a moon rock. The Planetarium, which also features science shows and laser concerts, is open Mon-Sat 9am-5pm and 7pm-9pm (phone 801-538-2098).

The **International Peace Gardens**, representing 14 countries, offer architecture, plants, and exhibits from nations around the globe. It's open May-November 8am-dusk (1000 South 900 West; phone 801-467-2592).

The **Lockerbie Collection** in the Science Hall of Westminster College at 1300 East and 1700 South showcases rocks and minerals. It's open Mon-Fri 8am-5pm (phone 801-488-4120).

The **Museum of Church History and Art** chronicles the history of Mormonism from 1820 to the present. Exhibits include sculpture and paintings from Mormons around the world. Open Mon-Fri 9am-9pm (45 North West Temple St., phone 801-240-3310).

The **Pioneer Craft House** at 3271 South 500 East St. was built in 1947 as a centennial project. The museum exhibits a collection of Utah arts and crafts. Open Mon-Fri 9am-3pm (phone 801-481-7131).

Pioneer Memorial Museum, 300 North Main, houses one of the West's most complete collections of 19th-century memorabilia. Four floors of the museum and a two-story carriage house display artifacts of Mormon pioneers, railroad and mining workers, and Native Americans. The carriage house contains early vehicles, including the wagon Brigham Young rode in when he entered the Salt Lake Valley. Guided tours, which last an hour, are available daily. The Museum is open year-round Mon-Sat 9am-5pm, and 1pm-5pm on Sunday from June to August (phone 801-538-1050).

Founded in 1862, when Abraham Lincoln ordered the California Volunteers to the Utah Territory to protect mail routes and assert Federal authority over the Indians, **Fort Douglas Military Museum** includes an impressive group of sandstone buildings from 1874 and a cemetery begun in 1863 and still in use. The Fort's museum depicts Utah's military history. Brochures for self-guided tours are available at the Museum. Open Tue-Sat 10am-4pm (32 Potter, phone 801-588-5188).

At the eastern edge of Fort Douglas, **Red Butte Garden and Arboretum** is Utah's premier botanical garden, with 150 acres of trees, shrubs, and floral displays. The Garden hosts concerts and special events in the summer, and free guided tours are available. It's open daily except Christmas from 9am-sunset (phone 801-581-5322).

The **Pioneer Trail State Park/This Is the Place Monument**, 2601 Sunnyside Ave., marks the western end of the 1,300-mile Mormon Trail with various displays. Next to the monument, a visitors center features an audio presentation and large murals on the Mormon migration. Open daily 10am-6pm (phone 801-584-8391).

In Liberty Park, whose pathways wind through beautifully landscaped grounds and around the Chase Mill, the **Tracy Aviary** supports over 240 species of birds. It's open daily 9am-6pm, and free bird shows begin at 1pm and 5pm Tue-Sun from Memorial Day to Labor Day (phone 801-596-0900). The **Chase Home Museum of Fine Art**, 589 East 1300, exhibits contemporary Utah folk art, including quilts, saddles, needlework, and woodcarving. During August, free concerts begin each Monday at 7pm. The Museum is open mid-April through mid-October from noon to 5pm daily (phone 801-533-5760).

At the **Utah Museum of Fine Arts**—the principal cultural resource for the visual arts in Utah—the collections range from ancient Egyptian pieces to superb examples of Italian Renaissance painting to modern American art. Other areas of the collection include Asian sculpture, Japanese prints, Chinese ceramics, Navajo textiles, and pre-Columbian artifacts. The Museum is open Mon-Fri 10am-5pm, Saturday and Sunday 2pm-5pm (phone 801-581-7332).

Some visitors to the **Great Salt Lake** come away disappointed. After all, there's not much foliage and no fish, and you can't drink the water. But those who take the time to investigate discover that the lake is a fascinating and starkly beautiful wonder of nature. On overcast days, the horizon of the lake blends into the sky, and the landscape assumes a surreal look, with the mountains and islands appearing to float in midair. On clear days, the sunsets over the lake can be breathtaking.

Since its discovery, the lake has been the object of myth and legend. Early settlers claimed to have seen a treacherous whirlpool in the center that afforded no possible escape. Another report describes a terrible lake monster with an enormous head. There's also been talk about a school of whales and a subterranean outlet to the Pacific Ocean. None of these stories has been substantiated.

The Great Salt Lake is actually the remainder of prehistoric Lake Bonneville, which covered 20,000 square miles in present-day Utah, Nevada, and Idaho. The four rivers and numerous streams that empty into the lake carry large amounts of dissolved minerals. Since the lake has no outlet, the minerals are trapped and create the high salinity, which ranges from 9% to 28% (compared to 3% in the ocean), depending on evaporation rates. Only the Dead Sea has a higher salt content. When the highest salinity occurs, the water has such buoyancy that swimmers can float in a standing position.

The lake is approximately 17 miles from downtown Salt Lake City on I-80; use exit #104. The Great Salt Lake Visitors Center, open Memorial Day to Labor Day from 9am-6pm, has an interpretive program to help travelers enjoy this unique natural wonder (phone 801-533-4083).

The **Bonneville Salt Flats**, just east of Wendover, Nevada off I-80, has been the site of hundreds of land speed records. The surface is smooth enough for high speeds, and there's enough water in the salt to keep tires from overheating and exploding.

In May, Salt Lake City holds a **Living Traditions Festival**, which features the culture of some 60 ethnic communities in the area. Food, entertainment, and craft demonstrations are available at the Salt Lake City and County Building. For details, call 801-533-5760.

The accommodating folks at the Salt Lake City Convention and Visitors Bureau have all kinds of brochures and information. They're at 180 South West Temple, Salt Lake City, UT 84101 (phone 801-521-2868).

SPRINGVILLE

First explored in 1776 by Father Escalante, a Jesuit priest, Springville was settled by eight families in 1850. It was first called Hobble Creek, because the pioneers often hobbled their horses there and left them to graze by the stream. The canyon stream has kept the name of Hobble Creek.

The town is home to the oldest, largest, and most beautiful art museum in Utah, the **Springville Museum of Art**, at 126 East 400 South St. This Spanish/Moroccan-style building houses remarkable works of art, including paintings by John Hafen and sculptures by Cyrus Dallin. Six galleries hold works by Utah painters and sculptors, and five galleries display temporary exhibits. The museum sponsors the **Art City Days Festival** each June, as well as a variety of dance and musical programs year-round. The free **Sunday Concert Series** features woodwind quartets, chamber ensembles, violin recitals, and vocalists, at 5pm in the Grand Gallery. The Museum's research library maintains the largest photo archive documenting the art of any state west of the Mississippi. Visitors are welcome to use this facility. The Museum is open Tue-Sat 10am-5pm and Sunday 2pm-6pm (phone 801-489-2727). Tours are available Tue-Fri 10am-4pm.

The **Daughters of Utah Pioneers Museum**, 175 South Main St., contains artifacts relating to the early Mormons. It's open Mon-Fri 9am-1pm, and on Wednesdays in the summer from 1pm-4pm (phone 801-489-4681).

Be sure to visit the **Kearns Hotel** at 94 West 200 South. This landmark hotel, built in 1892 and now on the National Register of Historic Places, has quite a colorful history. Turn-of-the-century Victorian decor and furnishings are still used.

At the **State Fish Hatchery and Game Farm**, visitors can observe the different procedures used in raising rainbow trout and pheasants. It's open daily 8:30am-4pm (1022 North Main St., phone 801-489-4421).

The Springville area offers many interesting annual events, starting with the Museum of Art's annual **Quilt Show** from early June through July (daily, 10am-5pm). June also brings **Art City Days**, with a parade, antiques show, fireworks, and a fun run. In early June, the **Historic Homes Tour** begins each half-hour starting at noon from the Museum of Art. In July, the **Springville Folkfest** features dancers and musicians from around the world. There's an admission fee for performances, but the opening parade, street dance, party in the park, and closing ceremony are all free.

The Springville Chamber of Commerce is at 175 South Main St., Springville, UT 84663 (phone 801-489-4681).

ST. GEORGE

St. George's heat and rocky terrain — difficult obstacles to the pioneers — are key elements in the natural mix that makes the area a great place to visit. Evidence of inhabitation of the area dates to the Anasazi culture over 1,000 years ago. Whites arrived when Brigham Young sent families there in 1861. The scenery didn't mean much to the early settlers, but today the views make the area a prime tourist destination.

Dinosaur tracks offer evidence of the enormous creatures that once roamed this area. In two spots near St. George, footprints left in mud ages ago were preserved until erosion exposed them. To get to the first site, which has been marked and interpreted by the Bureau of Land Management, you must negotiate several miles of dirt road. Take South Street east until it becomes River Road. (A map is available from the Chamber of Commerce in St. George.) The second site, near Washington

City (a few miles north of St. George), is more accessible. Turn north on Main Street at Nisson's Market, pass under the freeway, and find the dirt road that goes up the hill toward the water tank. Park at the tank and walk through the gate. Turn right again, walk northeast to a deep wash about 200 yards away, then follow the wash downstream. You'll soon see a slab of flat rock with dinosaur tracks.

Along the red bluffs north of St. George, **Pioneer Park** is the ideal spot for a picnic and a quick hike through mazes of sandstone mounds. Another intriguing natural spot is the forest of **Joshua trees** along Hwy. 91 west of the town. These "trees" are ancient cactus monuments named by the pioneers who passed this way over a century ago.

At **Snow Canyon State Park**, 10 miles west of town, canyon walls of red sandstone, volcanic cinder cones, and other formations resulted from a tremendous lava flow. Pictographs survive on the sandstone walls. A scenic route for mountain bikes covers about 24 miles from Ivins and runs through the winding canyon to the intersection of Hwy. 18, where it turns south to St. George. The park is always open.

Pine Valley, 32 miles north of town, is famous for its **Mormon chapel**. Built in 1868 by a shipbuilder, it's considered the oldest Mormon chapel still in use.

Hurricane, northeast of town, is the site of a historic canal built by its citizens in the early 1900's. The canal made water from the Virgin River available to land around the village, and some of the juiciest peaches in the world are now grown in the Hurricane area. Be sure to stop at the Hurricane Valley **Pioneer Heritage Park**, a beautiful square designed to depict the area's unique history. A central statue is surrounded by historical monuments and displays of pioneer artifacts like wagons and farm equipment. Each August, Hurricane celebrates **Peach Days** with a parade, contests, and lots of big, juicy peaches.

The historic **rock winery** at Toquerville, in the valley north of St. George, preserves a time when some Mormons became expert wine-makers, producing something they could easily trade with travelers.

The **St. George Mormon Temple**, the first completed west of Ohio, was built in the 1870's and is the oldest Mormon Temple in use today. The tabernacle supports a 140-foot steeple that serves as the town's landmark and is open to visitors. Guided tours explain Temple functions and Mormon beliefs. A brochure on a self-guided tour is available from the Chamber of Commerce (97 East St. George Blvd., phone 801-628-1658).

In Santa Clara, just west of town, the **Jacob Hamblin Home**, the circa-1863 residence of a Mormon missionary known for his peacemaking with the Indians, is open daily for tours. Indian grinding stones, separate living quarters for the wives, and a variety of pioneer artifacts depict life of a century ago. The home is open 9am-8pm daily (phone 801-673-2161).

Another historic home, the **Brigham Young Winter Home**, at 67 West 200 North St., has been restored with 19th-century furnishings. Guided tours run daily 9am-dusk from Memorial Day to Labor Day (phone 801-673-2517).

The **Daughters of the Pioneers Museum** displays memorabilia from St. George's early days, including a dress made from locally produced silk. Open Mon-Sat 10am-5pm (1143 North 100 East St., phone 801-628-7274).

This area is also a favorite with Hollywood producers, who have made dozens of films and commercials there. Butch Cassidy and the Sundance Kid rode their horses near the Virgin River; James Bond and Genghis Khan traveled through Snow Canyon; and Gary Cooper "Came from Cordura" across the dunes at Warner Valley. If you're lucky, you could get to watch a scene being filmed — or even work as an extra for a day.

A good brochure from the Color Country Travel Region describes various scenic drives and all the recreation available in the area. Contact them at 906 N. 1400 West St., St. George, UT 84771 (phone toll free 800-233-8824).

VERNAL

Vernal is nicknamed "Dinosaurland," conjuring visions of vast inland seas, great fern forests, and mighty beasts. The area's more recent history is also larger-than-life: Indians hunted there for centuries, waves of pioneers crossed the valleys, and outlaws hid in the remote canyons. Today, the Ute tribe and descendants of the pioneers live side by side. And thanks to earthquakes and erosion, the area's rich geologic history has been exposed, attracting scientists and tourists.

Mountains and water are important elements of this landscape. The Uinta Mountains are the highest in Utah and the only east-west range in the Western hemisphere. Winter snows blanket the peaks and melt in the spring, feeding sparkling streams that fill lakes, reservoirs, and tributaries of the Colorado River. The 2,000,000-acre **Ashley National Forest**, established by Theodore Roosevelt in 1908, covers this area with piñion pines and juniper. The **Drive through the Ages**, Utah's first designated scenic highway, runs from Vernal to the Wyoming border. The **High Uintas Wilderness** region ranges from Mirror Lake to North Pole Pass and contains hundreds of lakes stocked with trout. The mountain ridges divide the forest into scenic basins, and the floors are a spectacular contrast to the ridges, which abruptly rise thousands of feet. Since no cars are allowed, it's a great area for backpacking. The **Red Canyon Visitor Center and Overlook**, 40 miles north of Vernal, offers exhibits on the forest and magnificent views from 1,500 feet above the Canyon. It's open daily 9am-5pm from Memorial Day to Labor Day (phone 801-889-3713).

Record fish catches come from the waters of Lake Flaming Gorge, which forms the heart of **Flaming Gorge National Monument**, a potpourri of natural and human history, scenic contrast, and recreational opportunities. Exposed geologic formations represent a billion years of physical history; multi-hued soil and rock punctuate an essay of living color. The result is an array of flatlands, buttes, canyons, cliffs, slopes, and crags that support an abundance of plant and animal life. All of this surrounds the **Flaming Gorge Dam**, which rises 502 feet above bedrock and captures the waters of the Green River, creating a lake that extends 91 miles to the north. You can spot eagles' nests hundreds of feet above the water behind the dam, and bighorn sheep often appear on the rocky ledges. Numerous recreational facilities have been built along the lake. For

Viewing the bones at the Dinosaur Quarry Visitor Center.

more information, stop at the Visitors Center (phone 801-885-3135), where guided tours are available daily 10am-4pm from May-September.

The **Dinosaur Quarry Visitor Center**, 20 miles east of town, showcases dinosaur bones; many complete skeletons have been recovered nearby. Exhibits show the history of the quarry and explain the life and times of the dinosaurs buried in it. There's a charge for the monument itself, but the displays and an interesting audio-visual program at headquarters are free. Open 8am-4:30pm Mon-Fri (phone 801-789-2115).

The **Vernal Visitors Bureau** (235 East Main, Vernal, UT 84078; phone 801-789-6932) publishes brochures describing self-guided tours through the area's attractions. One of the most interesting is a drive to the **petroglyphs** in Dry Fork Canyon. Another tour leads to the **Jones Hole Fish Hatchery**, 40 miles northeast of town. The hatchery raises trout for lakes and reservoirs in Utah, Wyoming, and Colorado; you'll see indoor hatching pools with the fish in different stages of growth. A hiking trail connects the hatchery with the Green River, where an excellent trout stream emerges from a hole in the canyon wall. The hatchery is open daily 7am-3pm (phone 801-789-4481). Tour #9 is a walking tour of Vernal, including several museums. Don't miss the **Parcel Post Bank**, built with bricks mailed individually to Vernal. Back then, it was the cheapest way to get them from Salt Lake City to the town.

The **Daughters of the Utah Pioneers Museum** at 200 South and 500 West, contains artifacts and pictures of the area from the time the community was settled in the mid-1800's. Open Mon-Sat 1pm-7pm from June 1 to Labor Day.

The Ladies of the White House Doll Collection, on display in the Uintah County Library on Main St., includes dolls representing the country's First Ladies, each wearing a reproduction of the gown the woman wore at the Inaugural Ball. The Library is open 10am-8pm Mon-Thur, and 10am-6pm Friday and Saturday (phone 801-789-0091).

Thorne Studio, at 18 West Main, contains a photography and artifact collection from the Vernal area dating to the early 1900's. Open 10am-6pm Monday, Tuesday, Thursday, and Friday (phone 801-789-0392).

The **Western Heritage Museum** houses memorabilia from the county's "outlaw" past and other artifacts with a Western theme. An art gallery is also part of the facility (2nd South and 3rd West, phone 801-789-7399).

At the **Utah Field House of Natural History** (235 East Main St.), visitors stroll past 14 life-size dinosaurs displayed in a garden designed to look as it must have millions of years ago. The museum next to the garden has dinosaur fossils and Indian artifacts. It's open daily 9am-5pm (phone 801-789-3799).

The colorful history of the region is brought to life each summer during Vernal's **Outlaw Trail Festival** in June, with a trail ride, an outdoor musical, and a "shoot-out." The **Ute Indian Powwow** the first week in July has an Indian market, singing and dancing contests, and tribal ceremonies. The town's **Pioneer Days** festival starts with a huge parade in late July, and September brings the **Dina Soar Hot-Air Balloon Fest**. The **Christmas Festival** features the lighting of the Dinosaur Gardens, and thousands of tiny lights cloak the beasts in fantasy.

The **Ute Indian Tribe** lives on the vast Uintah Reservation amid snow-capped mountains, shimmering streams, high meadows, and lakes. Tribal lands, known for the abundant wildlife, offer excellent hunting and fishing. Licenses are available in Vernal. During the year, the tribe performs a variety of ceremonial dances, including the famous Bear Dance in the spring. Call 801-722-5141 for dates, which vary each year.

The **John Jarvie Historic Property** provides a fascinating glimpse of frontier life in an area still considered remote. About 40 miles northwest of Vernal, this 35-acre site preserves four original structures, each over 100 years old: a two-room dugout (the original house), a stone house built by outlaw Jack Bennett, a blacksmith's shop, and a corral made from railroad ties that had drifted down the river. The stone house is now a museum and contains the pole from which Jack Bennett was eventually hanged for his part in a local murder.

The General Store on the property, a replica of the original built in 1882, is furnished with many items from the period, plus the safe robbed the night of John Jarvie's murder. On July 6, 1909, Jarvie was robbed and killed, and his store was ransacked. His body, put in a boat set adrift on the Green River, was discovered eight days later. The killers were never captured. Visitors are always welcome, and tours run daily May-October from 10am to 5pm (phone 801-789-1362).

More Great Books
from Mustang Publishing

Europe for Free by Brian Butler. If you're on a tight budget — or if you just love a bargain — this is the book for you! With descriptions of thousands of things to do and see for free all over Europe, you'll save plenty of lira, francs, and pfennigs. **$10.95**
> *"Forget about American Express. One of these books is what you shouldn't leave home without!"* — *Toronto Sun*

Also in this series:
London for Free by Brian Butler. **$9.95**
Paris for Free (or Extremely Cheap) by Mark Beffart. **$10.95**
DC for Free by Brian Butler. **$9.95**
Hawaii for Free by Frances Carter. **$9.95**

France on the TGV: How to Use the World's Fastest Train to Get the Most out of France by Mark Beffart. Imagine boarding a train in Paris in the morning and arriving in Nice — almost 700 miles away — in time to get a suntan! With the TGV, the world's fastest train, it's easy, and this book describes everything you need to know to use this marvelous rail network. From descriptions of all the rail passes available to walking tours of over 50 French towns served by the TGV, it's a must for today's high-speed traveler. **$12.95**
> *"An exceptionally useful guide."* — *Atlanta Constitution*

Northern Italy: A Taste of Trattoria by Christina Baglivi. For the most delicious, most authentic, and least expensive meals in Italy, skip the *ristoranti* and head straight for *trattorie*, the small, unassuming cafés known only to locals. Describing over 80 *trattorie* from Rome to Milan, it's a must for the hungry traveler. **$12.95**
> *"The book's general premise is as sound as its specific eatery recommendations."* — *N.Y. Daily News*

The Complete Book of Golf Games by Scott Johnston. Want to spice up your next round of golf? With over 80 great betting games, side wagers, and tournament formats, this book will delight both weekend hackers and the totally obsessed. From descriptions of favorite games like Skins and Nassau to details on unusual contests like String and Bingo Bango Bongo, it's essential equipment in every golfer's bag. **$9.95**
"A must acquisition."—Petersen's Golfing

How to Be a Way Cool Grandfather by Verne Steen. Some things a grandfather just *ought* to know: how to make a sling-shot from an old limb and a rubber band, how to make a kite from a newspaper, how to do a few simple magic tricks, and how to make his grandchildren say, "Cool, Grandpa!" With complete details on making 30 fun, inexpensive toys, plus hints on using them to impart valuable lessons to kids, this is a great book for every old fogey who'd rather be way cool. **$12.95**
"A charming book."—The Spokesman-Review

The Complete Book of Beer Drinking Games by Griscom, Rand, & Johnston. With over 500,000 copies sold, this book reigns as the imbiber's bible! From classic games like Quarters and Blow Pong to wild new creations like Slush Fund and Beer Hunter—plus numerous funny essays, cartoons, and lists—this book is a party essential! **$8.95**
"The 'Animal House' of literature!"—Dallas Morning News

Mustang books should be available at your local bookstore. If not, send a check or money order for the price of the book, plus $3.00 shipping *per book,* to Mustang Publishing, P.O. Box 3004, Memphis, TN 38173 U.S.A. To order by credit card, call toll-free 800-250-8713 or 901-521-1406.

Allow three weeks for delivery. For rush, one-week delivery, add $3.00 to the total. *International orders:* Please pay in U.S. funds, and add $5.00 per book for Air Mail.

For a complete catalog of Mustang books, send $2.00 and a stamped, self-addressed, business-size envelope to Catalog Request, Mustang Publishing, P.O. Box 3004, Memphis, TN 38173 U.S.A.